John Dewey
PRIMER

PETER LANG
New York • Washington, D.C./Baltimore • Bern
Frankfurt am Main • Berlin • Brussels • Vienna • Oxford

Douglas J. Simpson

John Dewey
PRIMER

PETER LANG
New York • Washington, D.C./Baltimore • Bern
Frankfurt am Main • Berlin • Brussels • Vienna • Oxford

Library of Congress Cataloging-in-Publication Data

Simpson, Douglas J.
John Dewey primer / Douglas J. Simpson.
p. cm.
Includes bibliographical references and index.
1. Dewey, John, 1859–1952. 2. Education—Philosophy. I. Title.
LB875.D5S55   370'.1—dc22   2005035627
ISBN 0-8204-7136-4

Bibliographic information published by **Die Deutsche Bibliothek**.
Die Deutsche Bibliothek lists this publication in the "Deutsche
Nationalbibliografie"; detailed bibliographic data is available
on the Internet at http://dnb.ddb.de/.

Appreciation is expressed to several journal editors for permission to use previously published material, in particular "John Dewey's theory of the past, present, and future in the school curriculum," *The Review Journal of Philosophy and Social Science,* 29, 37–64; "John Dewey's view of grouping: A democratic perspective," *Educational Horizons,* 77 (3), 128–133; and "John Dewey's concept of the dogmatic thinker: Implications for the teacher," *Journal of Philosophy and History of Education,* 49, 159–172. In addition, a special word of thank you is extended to Southern Illinois University Press for permission to quote from *The Collected Works, The Poems of John Dewey,* and Dewey's November 1, 1894 letter to Alice Dewey. Finally, Michael J. B. Jackson, William Hull, Xiaoming Liu, Jacqueline Romano, and Jing Wang have our gratitude for the helpful suggestions they made on earlier drafts of this volume. The reference style used throughout this work is the one created by the staff of The Center for Dewey Studies, Southern Illinois University. For example, here the first piece of information, the date, (1894.11.01), indicates that the letter was written on November 1, 1894, and the latter (00218) is the number the staff assigned to the letter. References to *The Early Works of John Dewey, 1882–1898; The Middle Works of John Dewey, 1899–1924;* and *The Later Works of John Dewey, 1925–1953* are abbreviated as "EW" (early works), "MW" (middle works) and "LW" (later works). For instance, (MW 1: 5) indicates that the material cited or idea noted is in *The Middle Works,* volume 1, page 5. The feminine pronoun is used throughout this work to refer to both women and men.

Table of Contents

Introduction

Instrumentalism

the philosophical position that a warranted truth claim or knowledge is an instrument for future learning and for verifying other truth claims.

Progressive Education

the educational theory and movement in the late nineteenth and early twentieth centuries that emphasized the importance of and respect for children and their interests and experiences

John Dewey (1859–1952) is internationally known as a professor of philosophy and education. In fact, he is often considered the foremost American educational philosopher of the first half of the twentieth century. His approximately forty-year teaching career at the universities of Michigan, Minnesota, Chicago, and Columbia and the thirty-seven volume collection of his writings, *The Collected Works,* have secured for him an enduring scholarly influence. As one of the founders of philosophical **instrumentalism** and **progressive education,** he continues to be a reference point in many intellectual discussions. His collaboration with others to found the National Association for the Advancement of Colored People, the American Civil Liberties Union, and the American Association of University Professors signifies his commitment to civil, political, and academic freedoms and demonstrates that he was not merely an armchair philosopher but one who was involved in political and professional issues of freedom, equality, and justice.

Dewey, of course, continues to have many detractors in addition to proponents. His admirers range from true believers to reflective critics, and his attackers range from dogmatic ideologues to sophisticated scholars. The scope of agreement and disagreement with him includes questions that arise in his numerous political, educational, religious, ethical, aesthetical, ontological, epistemological, and psychological writings. His frequent speeches and prodigious writings on the controversial issues of war, discrimination, religion, equality, immigration, and schooling make it easy for a wide range of critics to attack his thoughts. His interest in the rights of women, children, diverse peoples, and employees distinguishes him from many of his contemporaries, too. The importance he placed on these and other issues, such as international affairs, economic issues, and educational development, resulted in visits to Mexico and a number of African, European, and Asian countries and extended his already considerable influence around the globe.

Given Dewey's academic and intellectual pursuits and accomplishments, the nature of his political and social involvements, and the extent of his international acclaim and criticism, it may seem peculiar, if not offensive, to refer to him as "an educational crank." The oddity of the phrase diminishes, however, when we realize that Dewey used the phrase in a letter to Alice (1858–1927), his first wife, to describe where he saw himself headed personally and professionally in 1894, his first year at the University of Chicago. The situations he observed in Chicago public schools led him to think educational conditions were terrible enough to make a person "howl on the street corners like the Salvation Army" [1894.11.01 (00218)]. While it is highly improbable that he ever literally howled on street corners about the educational needs of children and society, it is manifest that he criticized schools and society over a sixty-year period for failing to provide adequate educational environments and services. In 1894, the emerging educational activist

continued his letter to Alice by explaining his growing image of what a school could and should be. The needs of thousands of children, including Alice's and his—Fred (b. 1887), Evelyn (b. 1889), and Morris (b. 1892)—and his view of philosophy were motivating him to create an **experimental school** [1894.11.01 (00218)]. His activism on behalf of children and youths may have been stimulated by Fred, Evelyn, and Morris to a degree, but he clearly knew at least by 1899 that he could not stop with his interest in them. In fact, all of society—every parent if not adult—needs a more comprehensive passion for the development and education of children. In *The School and Society,* he stated:

Experimental school
the elementary school created at the University of Chicago to experiment with or test educational and psychological techniques, processes, and experiences

> What the best and wisest parent wants for his own child, that must the community want for all of its children. Any other ideal for our schools is narrow and unlovely; acted upon, it destroys our democracy. All that society has accomplished for itself is put, through the agency of the school, at the disposal of its future members. All its better thoughts of itself it hopes to realize through the new possibilities thus opened to its future self. Here individualism and socialism are at one. Only by being true to the full growth of all the individuals who make it up, can society by any chance be true to itself. (MW 1: 5)

By 1896, Dewey had moved forward with his image of what a school could be as he created the University Elementary School, later known as the Laboratory School or the Dewey School, at the University of Chicago. After the formation of this experimental school, he indicated that his own children turned his academic interests in the direction of philosophy of education (Mayhew & Edwards, 1936, 446). Several months after the Laboratory School was started, Dewey had an additional reason for developing a comprehensive philosophy of education when Gordon (b. 1896) was born. The births of Lucy (b. 1897) and Jane (b. 1900) and the addition of an Italian son, Sabino Piro Levis, in 1905 served to intensify and expand his interest in educational theory and practice (Martin, 2002). The for-

mal adoption of two Nova Scotia children, John, Jr. (b. 1942) and Adrienne (b. 1940), formerly Lewis and Shirley Hume, in 1948 by Dewey and Estelle Roberta Lowitz Grant Dewey (1904–1970), his second wife, at the ages of 88 and 44, respectively, came too late to significantly impact his educational philosophy but not too late for him to demonstrate his ongoing love for life and children (Simpson & Foley, 2004).

The Michigan Beginning

Although Dewey saw himself moving toward philosophy of education as a field of inquiry in 1894 as he settled at the University of Chicago, he had shown an interest in teaching, schools, and education much earlier. For example, he taught in high school in Oil City, Pennsylvania in 1879–1881 and at Lake View Seminary, Charlotte, Vermont in the winter of 1882. After attending Johns Hopkins University (1882–1884) and earning his Ph.D., Dewey accepted his first university appointment. At the University of Michigan (1884–1888), we find Dewey building on and using his educational experience and study of philosophy. Two early essays indicate that Dewey was interested in promoting both the education and health of women: "The Health of Women and Higher Education" and "Education and the Health of Women" (1885). Among other discoveries that he mentioned is the tongue-in-cheek claim that the average undergraduate female had much to learn about study habits from males regarding "the science of laziness" (EW 1: 73). Furthermore, the year before his son Fred was born he penned "Psychology in High-Schools from the Standpoint of the College" (1886) to discuss the merits of studying psychology in secondary schools, the aims of such study, and the means of teaching the subject (EW 1: 81–89).

In the 1886 essay, aspects of his later educational theory can be readily detected. Among other points, he argued against introducing the subject in high school in order to convey a particular system of psychology to students. Instead, he believed it should

be studied in order to cultivate open and flexible minds or to look at old ideas differently and new ideas honestly. Consequently, the test of successful teaching, according to him, is whether the student becomes intellectually alive and gains the ability to think for herself. The goal of education, therefore, is to develop "intellectual freedom, in its various factors of openness of mind, hospitality to ideas and ability to move among them unconstrainedly" (EW 1:87). His sense of humor is seen in this essay, too. If, he said, teachers of psychology—and other subjects—were effective in pursuing this goal, there would be fewer "monuments of blank and bland helplessness" enrolling in universities (EW 1:87). Indications of his future pedagogical thought also appeared as he claimed that the teacher should intimately understand each student's thinking and feelings, stimulate the student's capacity to discover for herself, and assist every child or adolescent as she appropriates and applies ideas (EW 1: 86–88). The next year (1887), he visited a number of nearby schools to examine how they functioned (Levine, 2001, 6–7).

The year after Fred (1887) and the year before Evelyn (1889) were born, Dewey conveyed the rudiments of his evolving ideas of ethics and democracy in "The Ethics of Democracy" (EW 1: 227–249). Noticeably, he argued against seeing democracy as the rule of a numerical majority or merely as a form of government. Instead, he believed that the heart of democracy is the means by which the thinking of the majority is formed and informed. Among these means are the needs to engage in widespread communication by peoples and to develop an understanding and valuing of the interests of diverse populations. Moreover, minority interests should be represented in public policy and in any democratic ethos that is built. Democracy, though, is more than a form of government; it is also a "form of society"—or as he would later say, a form of associated living (EW 1: 232). Interacting with and learning from one another and living in organic unity with common purposes are critical means of developing

and invigorating democracy as a form of social life. He concluded that governmental and societal democracy are tied together by the ethical, "Democracy, in a word, is a social, that is to say, an ethical conception, and upon its ethical significance is based its significance as governmental. Democracy is a form of government only because it is a form of moral and spiritual association" (EW 1: 240). Freedom, equality, and community were conceptions that informed his emerging democratic theory and eventually provided both a context and a means for his educational philosophy (EW 1: 240ff).

While Dewey had had a long-term interest in the idea of **experience**, it was at the University of Minnesota (1888–1889) that he declared that the most important question in philosophy is "What is experience?" (EW 3: 21). Initially, the question may not seem important but from his psychological, ethical, and philosophical perspectives, one's answer to the question indicates a great deal about her views of how we learn, understand, think, feel, appreciate, and develop. The rather innocuous term, therefore, held immensely important implications for him as an idealist philosopher and in the fields of learning, human development, and knowledge theory. In time, his interest in experience would gain additional significance as his educational theory evolved and he moved away from the Hegelian idealism he learned as an undergraduate student at the University of Vermont (1875–1879). Many years later as an instrumentalist, Dewey would conclude that a person's experience—unreflective and reflective, unexamined and examined, sporadic and holistic, and miseducative and educative—had profound implications for education, outside of and within the school. In *Experience and Education* (1938), he amplified the subject and delineated implications for schooling, teaching, and learning and the development of educated citizens. Among other emphases in the work, there is a highlighting of differences between educative, noneducative, and miseducative experiences. He claimed that the educative ones

Experience

the interaction of a person with objective environments in the process of living and learning; experience may be educative, miseducative or noneducative .

are those that we should focus on as educators, especially those involvements that enable students to enjoy interactive, continuative, and consummatory experiences (Simpson, Jackson, & Aycock, 2005, 132ff).

Before leaving Minnesota, John and Alice had their second child, Evelyn, who later coauthored with him *Schools of To-Morrow* (1915). While Evelyn was primarily responsible for selecting the schools examined in the volume, collecting data about them, and writing much of the book, Dewey's influence is obvious. The schools selected for study were those that were considered to reflect progressive educational theory in their everyday and experimental activities. Most of the schools were founded upon the ideas of theorists like Friedrich Froebel, Francis Parker, and Maria Montessori. Although neither the schools nor the theorists discussed are spared critiques by John and Evelyn, the practices mentioned indicate that Evelyn and John were at times more interested in describing contemporary schools than they were in evaluating them. Even so, Dewey's judgment of the importance of schools when compared with the broader educational environment is unmistakable. He claimed educators—and he probably should have added parents, policy-makers, and politicians—frequently forget

> What is learned in school is at best only a small part of education, a relatively superficial part; and yet what is learned in school makes artificial distinctions in society and marks persons off from one another. Consequently we exaggerate school learning compared with what is gained in the ordinary course of living. We are, however, to correct this exaggeration, not by despising school learning, but by looking into that extensive and more efficient training given by the ordinary course of events for light upon the best ways of teaching within school walls. (MW 8: 211)

Notice that he was interested in learning that occurs outside of school as well as the school's role in producing social classes. These two concerns appear throughout his extensive writings on education. Of

course, society at large contributes to the creation of classes as well as socializes people in other counterproductive ways.

A few years after returning to the University of Michigan (1889–1894), Alice and John's second son, Morris (1892), was born. Dewey's attention to educational questions, however, did not immediately and dramatically blossom. Instead his attention was largely focused on philosophical, ethical, and psychological issues. All of these interests, of course, contributed to his personal intellectual development that informed his emerging educational interests. Exceptions to this general scholarly emphasis existed, of course. In 1893, he completed "Teaching Ethics in the High School" in an effort to defend the value of teaching ethical inquiry in schools, even though many advised against such (EW 4: 54ff). He defended neither moralizing nor abstract reasoning in the teaching of ethics but instead encouraged teachers to present realistic case studies to students to get them to answer three questions about genuine ethical choices: Should they intervene in situations where distress is obvious? If so, how should they seek to relieve the distress? Finally, how should they decide what to do?

Dewey's cursory explanation of the teacher's role in the teaching of ethics is that she should build up the student's imaginative and sympathetic insight into human suffering by raising stimulating questions and making pertinent suggestions. The teacher's goal when teaching ethics, therefore, should be to have each student develop the habit of personally experiencing and understanding the realities of ethical thinking and decision making. Moreover, they should learn to sympathize with or understand the feelings of those who are personally involved in moral problems. In the process, students should be guided to look for the facts of a specific situation, search for the causes of the particular distress, examine the characteristics of the person in distress, discover the characteristics of generic human interactions, and weigh the options that are involved in the ethical rela-

tionship. He candidly concluded that the study of ethics can become more sophisticated than he described but that such depends in part upon the cultural context, the age of students, and the subject being studied. The third point—the subject being studied—raises the question of whether ethics should be a separate course of instruction or integrated into other forms of inquiry. With only a slight pause to consider the options, he recommended the second option. He refined this answer off and on throughout life but continued to promote an integrated curriculum.

This article by Dewey reveals theorizing that is a precursor to his later thinking about the teacher's specific pedagogical roles, the goals of teaching, the nature of learning, and the ideals of curriculum building. In particular, it indicates that the streams of thought that we find in his later educational philosophy were slowly emerging and that a kernel of his later theory of ethical reflection—termed *dramatic rehearsal*—is present. In his later writings, especially *Ethics* (MW 5), he added other important considerations, including the necessity of contemplating the probable consequences of our ethical choices or decisions. His ongoing inspection of schools during this time added to his firsthand knowledge of schools in Michigan and complemented his developing views of teaching, learning, and schooling (Levine, 2001, 10).

The Chicago Epiphany

When John and Alice arrived in Chicago, they had three young children: Fred, Evelyn, and Morris, approximately 2, 5, and 7 years of age. Soon they added Gordon (b. 1896), Lucy (b. 1897), and Jane (b. 1900). Their six children during the University of Chicago years (1894–1904) influenced Dewey's professional development in ways that his more academic engagements did not. Indeed, it is safe to say that Dewey's professional interactions were shaped in significant ways by his informal and formal study of child development as seen in Fred, Evelyn, Morris,

Gordon, Lucy, and Jane and other children. Home life was a laboratory for the study of children and theorizing about child development and learning. Sadly, the Deweys lost two of their children at early ages. Morris died in 1895 in Italy and Gordon in 1904 in Ireland while the family was vacationing. Alice and John were both traumatized by the deaths of Morris and Gordon and may never have completely recovered from the experiences.

In Chicago, Dewey immersed himself in family life, his professional responsibilities at the university, and the affairs of a rapidly changing multiracial and ethnic city. The city had the numerous challenges that an early twentieth-century urban setting did in those days, especially where there were great economic and educational disparities. Social, economic, and employment problems were significant if not critical. Thus, the city became his laboratory for the study of social, political, and economic quandaries. Dewey created the University Elementary School in 1896, as mentioned earlier, to study the learning and thinking of children. More precisely, he created an applied psychology or educational laboratory— or an educational laboratory based upon "a philosophical interpretation of psychology"—to explore the unity of knowledge as constructed by children who were guided by well-prepared teachers (MW 1: 67–68; LW 11: 202ff). Chicago, therefore, offered Dewey at least three laboratories: (1) a social, economic, and political laboratory in the city, (2) an educational laboratory in the school, and (3) a child development laboratory in his home. Little wonder, then, that he experienced a personal epiphany that resulted in a new focus on children, schools, society, and a comprehensive philosophy of education.

Given what Dewey saw and learned in Chicago, it is fortunate that he became an educational crank and that his philosophy of education took several major turns. Among his many developing interests were the nature of knowledge, the study of pedagogy as a university discipline, the preparation of future teachers, the relationship of educational theory and practice; the development of children and youths, and the psychological, ethical, and social dimensions of education. While a plethora of publications could be mentioned, illustrative educational works include "The Reflex Arc Concept in Psychology" (1896), "My Pedagogic Creed" (1897), "Ethical Principles Underlying Education" (1897), "The Psychological Aspect of the School Curriculum" (1897), *The School and Society* (1899), *The Educational Situation* (1901), *The Child and the Curriculum* (1902), "The School as a Social Centre" (1902), "Democracy in Education" (1903), and "The Relation of Theory to Practice in Education" (1904).

Two other works merit mentioning. First, there is the chapter "What Psychology Can Do for the Teacher" (1895) that appeared in *The Psychology of Number,* a volume he and James A. McLellan wrote. In this priceless chapter, he argued strenuously for a well-educated and reflective teacher who is a professionally autonomous educator, not a soldier who follows the orders of others. The professional teacher, so Dewey argued, is an artist who has great insight into students and their development in addition to understanding pedagogy and subject matter. A few years later (1901), he delivered a series of lectures at Brigham Young Academy—the forerunner of the university—that, if they were in book form, would equal the combined length of *The School and Society* and *The Child and the Curriculum.* In these frequently overlooked addresses, he discussed an assortment of educational themes, including learning theory, curriculum philosophy, child development, and character education. He delved too into the educational implications of such concepts as habit, play, attention, memory, judgment, and images. Of course, his earlier work titled "My Pedagogic Creed" (1897) is a marvelous delineation of and gateway to his philosophy of education at this period in his life.

The New York Experience

After a wearisome and, eventually, exasperating relationship with William Rainey Harper, the pres-

ident of the University of Chicago, Dewey resigned his position and accepted a new opportunity at Columbia University. His appointment was in the philosophy department, but he also had the opportunity to teach courses in Teachers College. Columbia provided him with an opening to return to full-time research and teaching, and he was pleased to leave behind the administrative duties of his department and the Laboratory School that consumed much of his attention in Chicago. In New York, his attention shifted immediately to philosophical pursuits as he wrote about, among other issues, knowledge, truth, reality, and warranted beliefs, but he occasionally wrote about educational and curriculum philosophy. In time, his attention refocused more to educational topics, including early childhood, industrial, and vocational education. Moreover, he explored in some depth the relationship of schooling and social issues, education and democracy, and academic freedom and education. Interested in the questions and concerns of his world, he wrote extensively about war, politics, workers, liberalism, communism, absolutism, and experimentalism. His lectures and research took him to a number of countries, including South Africa, Zimbabwe, Rhodesia, China, Japan, Mexico, Russia, and Turkey. He also wrote considerably on pertinent educational and political issues in other countries, especially China, Russia, and Turkey. While in South Africa in 1934, he spoke unequivocally about what he considered the principal social aim of education: "Unless the schools of the world can unite in effort to rebuild the spirit of common understanding, of mutual sympathy and goodwill among all peoples and races, to exorcise the demon of prejudice, isolation and hatred, they themselves are likely to be submerged by the general return to barbarism, the sure outcome of present tendencies if unchecked by the forces which education alone can evoke and fortify" (LW 9: 203–204).

During their early years in New York, John and Alice extended their family once again. This time they welcomed Sabino Piro Levis, probably seven or eight years old when they met him, later renamed Sabino Dewey (1905), into their home. They first saw Sabino while having lunch in a café in Venice, Italy. Inviting him to join them for lunch, they talked and later visited his mother. In a few days, they concluded that they wanted to adopt him and his mother concurred with their wishes. Remembering the context of Sabino's joining the Dewey household helps interpret this extraordinary event. Alice and John had lost two sons—Morris (1894) in Italy and Gordon (1904) in Ireland—while traveling in Europe, the former son in Milan. They, no doubt, were still suffering from the death of Gordon and being in Italy made it impossible for them to forget the passing of Morris, too (Martin, 2002, 234–235). Another uncommon experience occurred approximately fifty years later for Dewey. Near the end of his life, he and Roberta Dewey officially adopted two Nova Scotia children who were renamed John, Jr. and Adrienne Dewey. On this occasion, Roberta was more instrumental in initiating the adoption of John, Jr. before she and John were married in the fall of 1946. Later in 1948, she and John were involved in finalizing the official adoptions of John, Jr. and his older sister, Adrienne (Simpson & Foley, 2004).

By the time Dewey retired from Columbia in 1930, he had produced what are frequently considered his best works on education, including innumerable essays and several noteworthy books and monographs, e.g., *Moral Principles in Education* (1909), *How We Think* (1910), *Interest and Effort in Education* (1913), *Schools of To-Morrow* (1915), *Democracy and Education* (1916), and *Sources of a Science of Education* (1929). He also wrote dozens of entries for *A Cyclopedia of Education* (1911, 1912). Equally, if not more, impressive were his philosophical works: *German Philosophy and Politics* (1915), *Essays in Experimental Logic* (1916), *Reconstruction in Philosophy* (1920), *Human Nature and Conduct* (1922), *Experience and Nature* (1925), *The Public and Its Problem* (1927), *The Quest for Certainty* (1929), and *Individualism, Old and*

New (1930). Of course, Dewey did not divide his thinking into discrete realms, i.e., education and philosophy. His flow of thought moved easily and frequently from one topic to another because they were, in his mind, overlapping pieces of the same intellectual cloth. Philosophy and education, therefore, frequently commingle in his writings, although the weight given to one or the other subject is usually reflected in the titles of his writings. When studying his philosophy of education, it is expected that these two realms—philosophy and education—come together in his writings.

Dewey also wrote approximately a hundred poems, some complete and others incomplete, during his New York years, probably between 1910 and 1918. Although he never intended that the poetry be published, *The Poems of John Dewey* (Boydston, 1977) was released twenty-five years after his death. His topics range from children to nature to religion to philosophy to education to love. His love poems sometimes obliquely allude to his involvement with Anzia Yezierska Levitas, a coworker. At times, the poems focus on her to express his passions, reservations, and counterarguments during their eighteen-month affair in 1917–1918 (Boydston, 1977, xxii ff). Two poems that depict what Dewey liked least about educational practice and theory are titled simply "Education" and "To a Pedant." In the former piece, Education is personified and described as someone appealing and desirable, but who is kept from children by adults until they become capable of appreciating her. The time when children can approach and appreciate Education, however, never arrives according to their caregivers. In the latter poem, Dewey provided a glimpse into the mind of a pedant, perhaps the nadir of the educated person from his perspective. Both poems are stinging criticisms of traditional education views and remind one of Dewey's letter to Alice explaining that he was tempted to be an educational crank. Obviously, he yielded to temptation to be an educational maverick on many occasions.

After his formal retirement at age 70 (1930), Dewey remained at Columbia University for another decade and continued his speaking engagements and writing commitments as few people do during their so-called retirement years. From 1939 to 1952, the year of his death, he was professor emeritus of philosophy. Among his educational publications after his retirement are *The Way Out of Educational Confusion* (1931), *Education and the Social Order* (1934), and *Experience and Education* (1938). Furthermore, he wrote scores of short articles on educational issues, such as his piece titled "The Need for a Philosophy of Education" (1934). His philosophical writings included a more focused and in-depth discussion of his views of aesthetics and religion, e.g., *Art as Experience* (1934) and *A Common Faith* (1934). Other works, including *Liberalism and Social Action* (1935), *Logic: The Theory of Inquiry* (1938), *Freedom and Culture* (1939), *Theory of Valuation* (1939), and *Knowing and the Known* (1949), demonstrate his ongoing interest in both the affairs of society and the questions of philosophers. His essays also reflect the attention he gave to the nature of philosophy and its relevance to intellectual life, social challenges, and ordinary human affairs.

The Remainder of the Book

By now the different ways Dewey was inclined to become an educational crank may be somewhat clearer. Of course, he probably did not mean that by becoming a crank to become personally eccentric, odd, or strange. Even his detractors would not necessarily make this claim. Some might insist that his ideas are unfounded, dangerous, and stupid, perhaps, but usually not peculiar. Dewey himself, though, probably wished to suggest that he was inclined to become a professional crank in the sense that he would complain about or criticize existing educational philosophies, policies, and practices. He also implied that he was going to publicize his criticisms. His speeches and writings indicate that he howled in lecture halls, auditoriums, essays, and books rather than on street

corners. For his crankiness, many philosophers and educators are thankful. Many others probably wish that he had joined the Salvation Army, his confessed model, and delivered a different message to audiences.

As we examine Dewey's reasons for being an educational crank, we explore in later chapters a number of questions that take us into his reactions to the educational philosophies, policies, and practices that he observed. A few of these questions are as follows: Why do we cling to outdated views that dominate educational theory and practice? What are the educational ends or goals of schooling? Should we reconceptualize the experiences schools offer students? Should there be one curriculum or numerous curricula for students? What kinds of school environments should educators build? Are there better ways of promoting learning than those we find in both traditional and progressive schools? How is education related to both society and school? What does it mean to learn, think, and act? How should schools and society promote democracy? What kinds of people should schools in a democracy cultivate? When can we—teachers and students and others—claim to know? What are the roles of school and society in promoting a reflective life? Will democracy really work in schools? What are the basic emphases of democracy? How should teachers teach given our answers to the previous and related questions? In the following chapters, we explore these and other questions, in large part through Dewey's views about how schools should seek to encourage reflection and discourage dogmatism.

Glossary

Experience—the notion refers to the interaction of a subject (person) with objective environments (whether natural, social, or constructed) in the ongoing process of living and learning; it may be educative, miseducative, or noneducative.

Experimental school—a school created at the University of Chicago in order to experiment or test educational and psychological techniques, processes, and experiences.

Instrumentalism—the philosophical position that a warranted truth claim or knowledge is an instrument for future learning and for verifying other truth claims or propositions. See chapter 4.

Progressive education—the educational theory and movement in the late nineteenth and early twentieth centuries that emphasized, among other matters, the importance of and respect for children and their interests and experiences.

The Reflective Person

When examining Dewey's educational philosophy or theory, it is possible to begin with any number of topics, such as his theories of learning, teaching, and thinking. These ideas take us immediately into issues that are related to the everyday activities of the classroom teacher and student. Conversely, we could initiate this study with an examination of his largely unstudied theories of administration, organization, and supervision. These concerns transport us not only into realms of thinking, organizing, and behaving that significantly impact the means and outcomes of teaching and learning but also into practices that greatly influence the satisfaction and performance of the teacher and the student—or, as Dewey claimed, of the teacher-student (traditionally termed the teacher) and the student-teacher (customarily called the student). Alternatively, we might explore his thinking through such topics as curriculum, pedagogy, and assessment. These domains have direct and indirect implications for teaching and learning. His views of knowledge, values, and aesthetics

are also compelling, stimulating insight into educational practice, moral development, and art, theater, and music education. If we delve into his political and social philosophy, we also learn a great deal about the societies and communities—including schools and classes—that he believed provide a context for educative living and learning. A journey into his religious writings informs us of his own spiritual pilgrimage and what he thought could be a common religious experience. In all of these and other realms, his thought may be described—depending upon one's place in the philosophical and educational world—as radical, liberal, progressive, experimental, and, occasionally, conventional. His views, then, are open to multiple interpretations, especially if judged from present-day orientations. The interpretation we offer stems from an effort to understand what he seems to have said in his own context and how we might find implications in his ideas for contemporary educational concerns.

Recognizing the rewards of studying Dewey from the previously mentioned perspectives, we have selected still another approach that allows us to serendipitously explore his ideas, reaching into all of the aforementioned topics whenever desired. We begin with his conception of the reflective person. On this topic, he was unusually cranky about what went on in many schools and this explains why, at least in part, he wrote so much about reflective, experimental, and scientific thinking—all approximate synonyms for him. This portal to his educational theory moves us, in later chapters, into an analysis of democratic schools, school curriculum, knowledge claims, and ethical reasoning. How, in other words, did Dewey connect the curriculum, schools, knowledge, and ethics to the concept of a reflective person?

Reflective thinker
a person who is disposed to examine and evaluate the different grounds she and others have for believing and disbelieving truth claims, assumptions, and traditions.

Our approach to looking at Dewey's conception of a reflective person is, first, to explicitly introduce a few characteristics of the **reflective thinker.** Second, we spend time exploring the kind of thinker—the dogmatic person—that Dewey wished to discourage. As we do so, we simultaneously examine aspects of the qualities he wanted to encourage in a reflective thinker. Third, we turn to focus on the reflective person in a reflective society, a combination that Dewey encouraged educators to foster. Seeing these two sides of thinking—the reflective and the dogmatic—will ideally enable us to better understand the kinds of teachers we should consider becoming, developing, and employing and the kinds of students we should consider cultivating and graduating even when we disagree with Dewey's thinking. Finally, the conception of a reflective person is sprinkled in and clarified throughout this work, especially in chapter 4, where we explore Dewey's theories of knowledge and ethics.

One further notion needs to be mentioned. Dewey, from one angle, believed that one of the critical goals of schooling is the cultivation of reflective people, people who reflect upon and grow from their life and school experiences and who keep opening intellectual and other doors for themselves and others as long as they live. As teachers, he thought we *should*—note the ethical responsibility, not preferential option, in his idea—seek to nurture reflective students. The means of becoming a reflective person is in part by reflecting on what is being read, studied, heard, discussed, seen, and taught. So, in the case of promoting reflection, a *goal* of education for Dewey is also a *means* of learning and teaching. We move toward the goal of developing reflective thinkers by getting students involved in reflective thinking while they are in school. Keeping this idea in mind is useful whenever discussions of goals, ends, or aims and means, methods, or mediums are undertaken later.

The Characteristics of a Reflective Person

As we explore Dewey's idea of a reflective person, several strands of thought emerge, including but not limited to the person's

1   pursuing solutions to a problematic situation,
2   having a set of attitudes and dispositions that enhance the possibility and practice of reflection,

3 employing methods of inquiry that involve and promote reflection,

4 making a series of **judgments** that are intrinsically a part of reflection and

5 avoiding sets of beliefs, attitudes, dispositions, and practices that inhibit reflection.

Judgment

the activity of deciding which intellectual claims are based on relevant facts and arguments, their significance, and whether other considerations need to be made before making a decision

---

In this chapter, we concentrate on points (2) and (5) and discuss point (1) as required. Thoughts regarding point (4) are sprinkled throughout this chapter and in chapter 4. In chapter 4, we focus on point (3), methods of inquiry. Naturally, these five discussions do not—nor should they—always stay within the lines we have sketched but instead run over into one another.

While there are almost innumerable qualities, practices, and habits of a reflective person that Dewey interspersed throughout his writings, he synthesized many of these characteristics in *How We Think* (LW 8). Before he discussed these qualities, he clarified his general conception by affirming that reflective thinking is *"active, persistent, and careful consideration of any belief or supposed form of knowledge in the light of the grounds that support it and the further conclusions to which it tends"* (LW 8: 118). In order to be a reflective person, then, the student needs to be active not passive, persistent not irresolute, and careful not careless in her examination of beliefs and knowledge claims. Moreover, the student ought to learn to explore the grounds for truth claims as well as their consequences. Are the facts, reasons, and data for the claims open to public examination? If so, they need to be openly evaluated. What are the consequences of believing and acting on the particular claims? Are the claims instruments for more learning? Are they detrimental to the individual and society or do they lead to the growth of individuals and societies? In the process of reflection, the student needs to learn when there are sufficient grounds for believing and disbelieving truth and value claims. The motivating force behind this type of thinking and research is a desire to solve a problem, overcome a dilemma, address a doubt, or resolve an issue. As Dewey said,

"Thinking begins in what may fairly enough be called a forked-road situation, a situation that is ambiguous, that presents a dilemma, that proposes alternatives" (LW 8: 122). Some may wish to add that thinking often begins when we face multiple options, much like approaching a highway rotary that offers several alternatives to the thinker.

Dewey's statement that reflection entails "turning a subject over in the mind and giving it serious and consecutive consideration" stands out (LW 8: 113). Metaphorically, he suggested that thinking is much like mastication or chewing. We intellectually masticate as we turn ideas, information, data, and facts over in our mind. As we do so, we give serious, sustained, and systematic thought to how the evidence supports or discredits the assertions before us and how this supporting and/or discrediting allows us to reach a conclusion (LW 8: 114–115). Reflection, then, may take significant time and analysis.

In addition to being an active, persistent, careful, investigative, systematic, and ruminative thinker, Dewey said the reflective person is characterized by **open-mindedness,** *wholeheartedness,* and *responsibility* (LW 8: 135ff). This trio of qualities is needed to support the previously mentioned practices and should be developed along with them. *Open-mindedness* is a familiar if frequently misunderstood concept (Hare, 1985). For Dewey, it at least entails a "willingness to consider new problems and entertain new ideas" and includes "an active desire to listen to more sides than one; to give heed to facts from whatever source they come; to give full attention to alternative possibilities; to recognize the possibility of error even in the beliefs that are dearest to us" (LW 8: 136). Likewise, it includes an "alert curiosity and spontaneous outreaching for the new" (LW 8: 136–137).

Dewey's conception of *wholeheartedness, sincerity,* or *absorbed interest* may be partially hidden by his language (LW 8: 139). He called this characteristic both an attitude and disposition which results in the reflective thinker throwing herself into, focusing

Open-mindedness

an active disposition to listen, learn, and reflect on the ideas, facts, and arguments discussed by others

on, and being absorbed by a problem or issue. The idea overlaps with his earlier notion of persistence but extends it to include a "genuine enthusiasm" for a problem and its solution (LW 8: 137). Indirectly, Dewey was suggesting that the reflective thinker is devoted to and enjoys the pursuit of problem solving. In addressing real-life problems, the activity of reflection is as pleasurably embraced as it is seriously pursued. Part of the art of teaching, then, is helping students clarify and pursue genuine problems.

Responsibility is a word that suggests a concern for and commitment to present and future duties. Regarding the present, Dewey argued that without a sense of intellectual responsibility we are less prone to be open-minded and enthusiastic about learning and examining new information and data. The concept, therefore, indicates that we should move beyond intellectual consent to practicing what we say we believe. The reflective person experiences an intellectual and emotional agreement that leads to behavioral change (LW 8: 137–138). The future dimension of responsibility surfaces as Dewey discussed the consequences of a planned or actual action: "it means to be willing to adopt these consequences when they follow reasonably from any position already taken. Intellectual responsibility secures integrity; that is to say, consistency and harmony in belief" (LW 8: 138).

In summary, we have reached a preliminary view of Dewey's conception of the reflective person: She is an active, persistent, careful, investigative, systematic, ruminative, open, dedicated, and responsible thinker. She is moved by the conclusions she reaches to act both intelligently and ethically. We turn now to the sets of beliefs, attitudes, dispositions, and practices that inhibit reflection and to the causes of these factors. In the process, we notice the limitations that dogmatism places on an active and investigative mind or a mind that is characterized by openness to new information, absorption in solving problems, and responsible action based on the outcomes of reflection.

The Dogmatic Thinker

Two of Dewey's most respected books are *How We Think* (1933) and *Logic: The Theory of Inquiry* (1938). In these works, he described several kinds of desirable and undesirable thinking and the attitudes, disposition, and habits that are often associated with them. He also wrote of people who think in these different ways and described them according to the dominant traits and attitudes that he identified. For example, people are negatively described as uncritical thinkers (LW 8: 123), rudimentary thinkers (LW 8: 282), **empirical thinkers** (LW 8: 269), and **dogmatic thinkers** (MW 4: 188). His preference for reflective thinkers—while not unchallengeable—is understandable when compared to the other options he described.

His concentration on the reflective person is reasonable, too, if we assume that it is more important to understand and practice reflective thinking than it is to understand and avoid flawed types of thinking, including dogmatic thinking. Of course, studying one of the two sets of activities—reflective thinking *or* dogmatic thinking—easily leads into an understanding of the other. Ideally, for instance, engaging in reflective thinking diminishes dogmatic thinking. However, one may argue that understanding and avoiding dogmatic thinking enhance reflective thinking in ways that studying reflective thinking alone—if such is possible—does not. Thus, studying either kind of thinker probably advances our understanding and development as a reflective thinker. Understanding the practices, attitudes, and dispositions that Dewey wanted educators to discourage may, therefore, help us facilitate an understanding and practice of those desirable qualities he wished to nurture. In pursuing this understanding, we examine his comments about the prevalence of the dogmatic mind, its causes, its nature, and its offspring, i.e., dogmatic education.

Empirical thinker

a person who typically engages in thinking that is based largely on unexamined and unreflective personal experience

---

Dogmatic thinker

a person who feels and thinks that certain assumptions, ideas, and facts are permanently settled and that they do not need to be reconsidered for clarification, revision, or rejection

The Prevalence of the Dogmatic Mind

To appreciate the import of Dewey's objections to dogmatic thinking, we need to recognize his resolute opposition to the dogmatic tendencies he identified in individuals, schools, and society. We note, to begin with, that Dewey spoke scathingly of *dogmatic opinions and ideas,* regardless of whether they were assumptions (LW 4: 146), preconceptions (LW 11: 440), beliefs (MW 4: 176), convictions (LW 10: 323), assertions (MW 13: 57, 321), or denials (MW 13: 57, 221). He opposed dogmatism regardless of whether a person argues for or against a position and whether it shows up in discussions of art (LW 1: 282–283), moral development (MW 11: 348), history (LW 11: 61), politics (MW 3: 200), or pedagogy (MW 13: 321). He also noted that dogmatic opinions may arise in connection with scientific (LW 6: 275), theoretical (LW 7: 317), and democratic claims (MW 13: 338). In *A Common Faith,* he pointedly stated that "There is no special subject-matter of belief that is sacrosanct" (LW 9: 27). Not only are there no privileged intellectual domains that can claim that they are immune to dogmatism, there are no privileged interpreters or voices that are unquestionably correct. There are neither old nor new voices or paradigms that are untouchable or advantaged, including Dewey's own philosophy.

Dewey's harshest words may be directed at dogmatic social, political, and religious philosophy (MW 12: 222). He described many absolutists (LW 16: 355), socialists (LW 6: 170), and Marxists (LW 11: 439) as dogmatists and declared that materialism (MW 2: 194), positivism (MW 2: 209), skepticism (MW 2: 234), rationalism (MW 7: 220), fundamentalism, (LW 5: 72), progressivism, and traditionalism (LW 13: 9) are—or at least can be—dogmatic systems of thought. His objections to the dogmas of communism, for instance, were based on their being "as fixed and unyielding as that of any church" (LW 5: 356) and resulted in a political faith that is an unthinking one (LW 9: 92). Thus, he strongly warned of dogmatic attitudes (MW 12: 262), habits of mind

(LW 8: 124), and habits of thought in any philosophy (LW 9: 27).

We are well-advised to mention—and get a little ahead of ourselves—several aspects of Dewey's theories of truth, logic, and reflection. This early visit to these topics is justified in view of his belief that the dogmatic person has answered with finality her questions about some, many, or, even, most issues. She has formed an opinion, made up her mind, and settled questions *permanently*. She neither sees a need for nor wishes to revisit certain topics or issues. For example, the dogmatist might adamantly insist that Piaget is dead and Vygoysky is alive; modernism is garbage and postmodernism is manna; ethics of justice is essentially a male-contaminated rationale for the status quo and ethics of care is basically female-tainted relational ideologies; eastern ideas are rooted in irrationality and mysticism and western ideas are based on positivistic and rationalistic abstractions; cultural insiders alone can understand issues and cultural outsiders always distort them; direct instruction theories are impositional and demeaning and facilitative pedagogical theories are liberating and respectful. These and numerous other questions may be settled for the pedagogically dogmatic mind. Nothing is left to learn about or from either side of the dichotomized and polarized positions. Why reopen an issue when the whole truth is already known? In contrast, the reflective teacher and student are open-minded about examining new evidence, data, and interpretations and revisiting long-standing questions from different perspectives. The dogmatic teacher burrows a permanent home into an ancient, medieval, or contemporary ideology while the reflective teacher seeks to construct her home by deconstructing the pedagogical orthodoxies and heterodoxies she encounters. Her unending construction leads to many reconstructions of her intellectual and professional home.

The dogmatic mind influences us in other ways, too: even so-called non-controversial subjects may

be settled in such ways that we are kept from examining new information, different interpretations, or alternative understandings. Dewey countered this inclination with the spirit of an experimentalist in *Logic: The Theory of Inquiry:*

> The "settlement" of a particular situation by a particular inquiry is no guarantee that *that* settled conclusion will always remain settled. The attainment of settled beliefs is a progressive matter; [and] there is no belief so settled as not to be exposed to further inquiry. It is the convergent and cumulative effect of continued inquiry that defines knowledge in its general meaning. In scientific inquiry, the criterion of what is taken to be settled, or to be knowledge, is being *so* settled that it is available as a resource in further inquiry; not being settled in such a way as not to be subject to revision in further inquiry. (LW 12: 16)

Notice several ideas Dewey mentioned. First, a settled issue may not always remain settled. Second, issues become settled progressively, over a period of time, not instantaneously. Third, no belief is so settled that we can be sure that it will not be reexamined and, perhaps, rejected in the future. Fourth, knowledge in general emerges from ongoing inquiry and because of a cumulative convergence of facts or data. Fifth, any claim that deserves the title scientific knowledge is so settled that it can be used for further inquiry. That is to say, scientific knowledge is so secure that it can be used as an instrument to engage in additional investigations. Sixth, a settled issue may be revisited and our answer to it reconsidered as we determine whether our ideas should be retained, revised, or rejected. In this context, the idea of someone having a particular mind*set* takes on new meaning, e.g., she is unlikely to rethink her opinions, conclusions, or beliefs. Conversely, the reflective person is willing, if not eager, to revisit, rethink, and revise her thinking as new perspectives and evidence suggest.

Scientific thinker

a person who emphasizes the importance of studying issues from a scientific or reasoned position

Two observations are in order. First, Dewey used the words *scientific thinking* (hence **scientific thinker**) to refer to reasoned or reflective approaches to exam-

ining evidence and arguments. The meaning of the words is roughly equivalent to reflective thinking and is not limited to social and natural science research. Second, his use of the term *logic* deviates from the standard way many philosophers employ the term. In his opinion, logic is neither a branch of mathematics nor the study of propositions. Rather, logic is a study of "how we think," particularly when we are doing it well and are successful thinkers. The experimental or scientific method of examining issues leads to "hypotheses directive of practical operations, not truths or dogmas" (LW 12: 505).

Why, we may ask, given Dewey's admiration for democracy, confidence in education, and faith in humanity, did he believe that dogmatic thinking is so prevalent and reflective thinking so uncommon? His answer involved, in part, his understanding of philosophical anthropology, evolutionary science, and social theory. If his explanations are defensible or even insightful, they may assist us as we go about our responsibility to develop reflective students. If not, examining his ideas may help us develop our reflective abilities at his expense.

The Causes of the Dogmatic Mind

Identifying causes is a risky, sometimes perplexing endeavor. The difficulty is partially attributable to the complexity of causation and is compounded by the fact that some people interpret causes in a mechanistic fashion. Identifying causes is also difficult because we interpret them through particular lenses and offer explanations that are to some extent perception determined, because, as Dewey noted, no one brings a virgin mind to any intellectual problem (LW 8: 214). Consequently, his view of seeing and understanding, including his epistemology, may be described as perspectivist: The perspective of the seer or thinker invariably influences what is seen, considered, and believed. Even so, his view of **perspectivism** or perspectivalism is not always straightforward or simple. He believed we can move beyond a complete perspectivism by means of reflective or scien-

Perspectivism

the theory that a person's thinking is either partially or completely determined by her context, experience, and philosophy

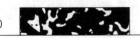

tific thinking: A person need not be absolutely or totally restricted or blinded by prior experiences and beliefs. Instead, by critically evaluating one's assumptions and perspective by interacting with others, a person can become open to different ways of seeing and seeing her own views differently. She can change her mind about even basic beliefs and cultivate inter- and cross-perspectival understandings. In other words, she need not remain a complete outsider to all ideas other than her own views regardless of whether they are long-standing or newly acquired beliefs. In part, the point of becoming reflective is that the person is "reborn into the life of intelligence" and is, with appropriate study and interactions, better able to recognize and, thereby, address the detrimental features and utilize the positive aspects of personal perceptions (MW 15: 7). During a lifetime of growth as a reflective thinker, a person should develop a broader, richer, more inclusive and warranted perspective, although her way of seeing will remain partially shaded by her old or new lenses. Lifting the shading lenses, therefore, may begin with and be aided by identifying our own dogmatic tendencies and their causes. The lenses, though, need not necessarily be completely discarded, because they may help us see things that others do not.

Dewey attempted to promote a reflective mind, then, by identifying multiple causes of dogmatic thinking: natural inclinations, cultural conditions, emotional needs, unsettling circumstances, instinctive tendencies, organizational success, and empirical thinking. First, he suggested that there are natural propensities as well as cultural conditions that influence people to avoid thinking reflectively. For example, he complained of an either-or thinking propensity: "Mankind likes to think in terms of extreme opposites. It is given to formulating its beliefs in terms of Either-Ors, between which it recognizes no intermediate possibilities" (LW 13: 5). He also said that there is a "primitive credulity" and "a natural tendency to believe anything unless there is overpowering evidence to the contrary" (LW 8: 130). Likewise, he argued that natural inclinations drive people to irrational, unscientific thinking and that such thinking seeks "the crutch of dogma" to avoid "the trouble of thinking and the responsibility of directing . . . activity by thought" (MW 9: 348–349). The reflective thinker, on the contrary, has developed the inclination and ability and accepted the responsibility to think rather than merely refer to some previously developed belief in an effort to settle issues. She also rejects the tendency to avoid the intellectually "unpleasant" (LW 8: 197).

Dewey, nevertheless, was not dismayed by what he called natural propensities and argued, "If human nature is unchangeable, then there is no such thing as education and all our efforts to educate are doomed to failure. For the very meaning of education is modification of native human nature in formation of those new ways of thinking, of feeling, of desiring, and of believing that are foreign to raw human nature" (LW 13: 292). An educative environment and reflective teacher, though, can guide students, foster their reflective thinking, and modify human nature (LW 13: 292). However, we should not be naïve: Environments may have a positive effect or a negative one or a mixture of the two. In fact, Dewey identified several environmental factors that influence people to be dogmatic and observed that living in an unpredictable, even precarious, world compels people to look for security. He argued that "perfect certainty" is what we want (LW 4: 17, 32), in part, because we have a "need for security in the results of action" (LW 4: 32). This need for predictable actions and consequences, therefore, easily leads to "acceptance of dogmatic rules as bases of conduct in education" (LW 4: 32). As a consequence, traditional thought—because it is largely or completely settled—contributes to the growth of dogmatism (LW 8: 271). As educators, we may wish to ask ourselves whether we are inclined to welcome dogmatic rules, regulations, and practices because we are experiencing unsettling times in our lives, profession, and society. Similarly, we may wish to ask if our stu-

dents live in unsettling circumstances and live in ways that influence them to become more dogmatic and less reflective. Should, we may inquire, our answers to these questions alter our pedagogy?

For Dewey, then, it appeared clear that the desire for certainty, the presence of unpredictable environments, and the force of human nature collaborate to push a person toward dogmatic thinking. He elaborated on these forces and added another—the tendency to confuse a feeling of certitude with a public rationale for certainty—when he wrote about how dogmatism may lead to intolerance, fanaticism, and irresponsibility:

> Tendency to premature judgment, jumping at conclusions, excessive love of simplicity, making over of evidence to suit desire, taking the familiar for the clear, etc., all spring from confusing the feeling of certitude with a certified situation.
>
> Thought hastens toward the settled and is only too likely to force the pace. The natural man dislikes the dis-ease, which accompanies the doubtful and is ready to take almost any means to end it. Uncertainty is got rid of by fair means and foul. Long exposure to danger breeds an overpowering love of security. Love for security, translated into a desire not to be disturbed and unsettled, leads to dogmatism, to acceptance of beliefs upon authority, to intolerance and fanaticism on one side and to irresponsible dependence and sloth on the other. (LW 4: 181–182)

It is easy to see why Dewey concluded—whether we concur or not—that "the mass of people refuse to look facts in the face and prefer to feed on illusions" (LW 9: 77). In spite of that, he was optimistic that education can make a difference in the way people face facts and, indeed, even determine what the facts are in specific situations.

Even in better circumstances, however, Dewey concluded that people may be influenced to think dogmatically. Successful leaders may nurture a cult of the "infallibility of leadership" and, thereby, cultivate dogmatism in their organizations (LW 9: 91). Even great thinkers may have their imaginative thoughts "frozen" in time by those who admire their ideas and may eventually have their creative insights turned into "dogma" (LW 13: 320). Moreover, Dewey maintained that "empirical thinking"—*not* scientific thinking, but *ad hoc* thinking rooted in uncritical personal experience—has three basic disadvantages, including its "most harmful" tendency to "engender mental inertia and dogmatism" (LW 8: 270). In turn, he said that intellectual "laziness, unjustifiable conservatism" are the likely companions of dogmatism (LW 8: 270). Why, we may be tempted to ask, did Dewey associate intellectual laziness with dogmatic thinking? Recall his earlier statement that dogmatism may lead "to acceptance of beliefs upon authority, to intolerance and fanaticism on one side and *to irresponsible dependence and sloth on the other*" (LW 4: 181–182; emphasis added). In the end, he connected dogmatism and laziness because he believed that the truly dogmatic thinker puts little effort into genuine learning or thinking about the particular subject or topics that she has turned into dogma. She has a closed mind. Issues that are settled do not require attention or effort.

Finally, Dewey believed that people may tend to be dogmatic because our experiences are not informed by discussions with people who have different experiences. He asserted that when personal experience excludes the experiences of others, it nurtures dogmatism:

> Dogmatism, adherence to a school, partisanship, class-exclusiveness, desire to show off and to impress, are all of them manifestations of disrespect for experience: for that experience which one makes one's own through sympathetic intercommunication. They are, as it were, deliberate perpetuations of the restrictions and perversions of personal experience. (LW 6: 21)

Associating largely with friends who have similar experiences and understandings, therefore, may lead to dogmatism if Dewey is correct. For instance, pragmatic, critical, identity, feminist, or positivistic theoreticians who associate primarily with one another, may be inclined to immediately disrespect the experiences and ideas of those who think otherwise. So,

too, children who interact mostly in monocultural, religious, intellectual, political, social, and linguistic settings, may be disinclined to consider the thoughts of those from multicultural and pluralistic environments. Instructionally speaking, then, placing students in diverse learning groups is worth considering for more than one reason.

If dogmatism is as debilitating as Dewey claimed, but largely avoidable if societal and school conditions are educative, we seem to need to understand more than its dangers and etiology. A request for a clarification of the nature of dogmatic thinking, then, seems reasonable: What does it mean to be a dogmatic thinker? What kinds of thinking should educators and schools discourage? While we have already partly addressed these questions, we now concentrate on them.

The Nature of Dogmatic Thinking

Writing early in life, Dewey indirectly revealed criteria for understanding the nature of both dogmatic and reflective thinking—and probably the nature of the dogmatic thinker, too. He wrote:

> It is hardly necessary, I suppose, to profess the deepest respect for the Golden Rule, but this is not inconsistent with recognizing that if it were not held open to reflective criticism, to analysis of meaning and bearing, it would surely degenerate into a mere external command. That it, or any other rule, may be a workable tool, that it may give aid in a specific case, it must have life and spirit. What can give it the life and spirit necessary to make it other than a cramped and cramping petrification except the continued free play of intelligence upon it? (EW 3: 101–102)

In this quotation, he attributed four qualities to the kind of thinking he later called dogmatic:

1   it does not allow reflective criticism of cherished beliefs;
2   it does not allow ongoing analysis of ideas for their meaning and applicability;

3   it does not nurture a reflection on highly prized rules;

4   it has a petrifying influence on intelligence.

Conversely, he believed that reflective thinking was consistent with holding a respect for rules of conduct if the rules are viewed as tools for thought, involve an open examination of our most revered beliefs, and entail a free interaction with relevant ideas and data. Later, he stated his preference for the terms *principles* and *concepts* to the word *rules* when discussing ethical questions (LW 7: 275).

Writing at the University of Michigan, Dewey revealed more of his thinking about dogmatism, religion, and philosophy when he argued that every aspect of life is a legitimate field of investigation for the philosopher. He also suggested a line of division between doing philosophy or scientific inquiry and thinking dogmatically: "As soon as any fact of life is said to be outside scientific investigation, philosophy is no more and dogmatism has begun" (EW 4: 366). He quickly inserted that the philosopher cannot set "aside any portion of life which he says is entirely beyond further interpretation and knowledge" (EW 4: 366). In this comment, he identified the grounds for positions he later developed more fully. He believed, for instance, that certain claims, particular kinds of propositions or assertions—such as, first, this belief is beyond the scope of reflective inquiry; second, there is nothing new to learn about this subject, and, third, there are not any other legitimate interpretations of this matter—are rooted in dogmatic thinking. Alternatively, reflective thinking welcomes—indeed, involves—critical thinking, the opportunity to learn and examine diverse interpretations of data.

Dewey further alleged that the nature of some dogmatic thinking involves the multiplication of conceptual distinctions within dogmas, apparently to build intellectual walls to protect beliefs from criticism (MW 1: 155), and he implied that there are degrees and different kinds of dogmatic thinking. Some thinking constitutes "undue dogmatism" (MW 2:

58) or is "dogmatic in the extreme" (MW 1: 155). He also used such adjectives as "old" (LW 4: 153), "rigid," "authoritative," "irresponsible and indiscriminate," "absolute," "traditional" (MW 12: 163–171), "harsh" (LW 1: 322), and "dead" (LW 17: 530) to describe dogma and dogmatic thinking. These words may reflect nothing more than a rich vocabulary or they may reflect the fact that Dewey sensed that some dogmatic thinking is more inflexible, antiquated, insensitive, and arbitrary than other types. The observant educator, no doubt, will be able to use these possible interpretative categories as she seeks to understand classroom and private discussions.

In addition, Dewey described what may be viewed as the developmental nature of dogmatic thinking. His own words are that an idea may sometimes "harden" into dogma (LW 17: 528) and that "old knowledge" may degenerate into "dogmatic doctrines" (MW 12: 98). When ideas devolve into dogmas, of course, the result is fixity of ideas (MW 1: 157). In time, a person's dogmatic thinking may devolve beyond specific, isolated beliefs into a "closed system," a position that is both comprehensive and resistant to external questioning (MW 2: 295). Recognizing this potential devolution may help us intervene at strategic points in a student's development as we teach.

Perhaps in anticipation of more recent accounts of the blinding effects of a person's perspective, Dewey described the dogmatic thinker as a person who protects her beliefs and view of herself from unsympathetic ideas and interpretations. Likewise, she uses her "closed system" to give a "prompt interpretation" of new arguments (MW 4: 119), refuses to use her intelligence in evaluating personal beliefs (MW 7: 61), upholds her position regardless of the intellectual costs (MW 13: 34), and refuses to make causal connections that are antithetical to her own system of thought (MW 8: 140). Ultimately, it is clear why Dewey applied what he said about religious dogmatists to non-religious ones:

It is the essence of all [both sacred and secular] dogmatic faiths to hold that any such "showdown" [the testing of claims by "common tests"] is sacrilegious and perverse. The characteristic of religion, from their point of view, is that it is—intellectually—secret, not public; peculiarly revealed, not generally known; authoritatively declared, not communicated and tested in ordinary ways. (MW 4: 172–173)

Dewey's extensive description of the nature of dogmatic thinking went farther. Arguing against the tendencies of certain communists and tenets of communism in "Why I Am Not a Communist," he made a couple of provocative distinctions between the dogmatic and the reflective thinker. On the one hand, he implied that the nature of dogmatic thinking was so powerful that a person could not examine the facts without "changing [them] . . . to suit . . . special purposes" (LW 9: 92). On the other hand, the reflective person's thinking was characterized by "fair-play, elementary honesty in the representation of facts and especially of the opinions of others" (LW 9: 94). He insisted that these qualities—fairness and honesty in looking at facts—cannot be simply dismissed as "bourgeois virtues" (LW 9: 94). Turning to educators, he argued that the reflective mind needed to be cultivated along with the learning of information in schools. Students needed to be brought to the point that they "adopt into the very make-up of their minds those attitudes of open-mindedness, intellectual integrity, observation and interest in testing their opinions and beliefs that are characteristic of the scientific attitude" (LW 9: 99). A positive sign for a reflective thinker, therefore, is when she represents ideas that she detests the way a proponent would characterize them. That is, she is fair in her description of the views of others.

Dewey later shifted his emphasis from the way a person holds a specific belief to a person's disposition toward beliefs in general and her unquestioning or uncritical attitude toward life. For instance, he elucidated the idea by combining the word *dogmatic* with other terms, such as "dogmatic and uncriti-

cal" (LW 1: 303) and "fixed and dogmatic" (LW 2: 8). Moreover, he reiterated that the dogmatic thinker is likely to hold to "unexamined fundamental premises [and] unquestioned assumption[s]" and added that she may be "hostile to the theories" that run counter to personal beliefs (LW 3: 319). He also picked up the idea of a "dogmatic attitude" again (LW 2: 8) and referred to the "hopelessly committed" (LW 3: 305), implying that there are emotional inclinations and attitudinal tendencies which support the intellectual tendencies of some dogmatic thinkers.

His concern for dogmatism may offer a gestalt when we place his comments in the context of his overall thinking. He speaks of "an unquestion*ing* dogmatism" (LW 7: 268; emphasis added) that seems to suggest that not only do dogmatic thinkers not allow others to question their opinions but that they do not question them either, implying that dogmatic thinkers are not inclined to live an examined life. In this case, the idea that dogmatism is fatal to inquiry takes on a double meaning: The intellectual lives of both the friendly inquirer and the committed dogmatist are damaged (LW 16: 325), the former because she is not allowed to question and the latter because she is not willing to inquire. Unhappily, the thinking of the dogmatist in this situation cannot be modified as long as she refuses to question her beliefs (LW 10: 46), and she is, therefore, without the intellectual power for further growth (LW 10: 62–63).

However, it is not only individuals' intellectual lives that are in question. Dewey believed that dogmatism, like skepticism, is an emotional indulgence that serves neither the individual nor society well (LW 4: 182), and that it arrests "choice of means" (LW 13: 321). Why, we may wonder, did Dewey think that skepticism and dogmatism are emotional indulgences? Are we to believe that there is something undesirable about skepticism, too? Being skeptical at times is definitely admirable in the minds of many people, as it was with Dewey. Even so, being uniformly, continuously, and invariably skeptical about the possibility of gaining any knowledge whatsoever has several problems, including the idea that it is a negative form of dogmatism and undermines the foundation to inquiry. Why search for understanding if we *know* absolutely that we can never *know* anything? Dewey had no appreciation for either absolute skepticism or dogmatism, then, because he was interested in learning, thinking, questioning, and understanding (LW 4: 182ff).

We return briefly to his idea of how dogmatism, including absolute skepticism, limits choices of means or curtails learning: "All dogmatism is by its nature an economy of scarcity, scarcity in forming a hypothesis and entertaining alternative ideas. Any liberal creed, on the other hand, must be an economy of abundance in a freedom of developing hypotheses" (LW 17: 444). Absolute skepticism offers basically one dogmatic hypothesis: We can never know anything. For Dewey, the hypothesis was as untenable as the dogmatic hypothesis that we can know absolutely the truth about any issue.

The Dogmatic in Education

In his well-known statement on the nature of the dogmatic thinker in *Experience and Education,* Dewey argued against the weaknesses of both progressive and traditional education, noting that either can be based on dogmatic thinking. He stressed that the problem is not pedagogical belief *per se* but how a belief is held and the attitude and disposition behind the holding that are informative. A dismissive, sneering, or condescending response to the ideas of others may exhibit the attitude of which Dewey warned. The dogmatic thinker, in short, is any person—whether a traditionalist or a progressivist—who holds determinedly and forcefully to her beliefs and is not inclined to dialogue about her most prized opinions and practices: "For any theory and set of practices is dogmatic which is not based upon critical examination of its own underlying principles" (LW 13: 9).

Dewey's concern about the potential of dogmatism in progressive and traditional schooling appeared

Closed Orthodoxy

a point of view that assumes that all philosophical, scientific, religious, or educational questions have been answered without the possibility of revising the answers in the future

elsewhere, too. He counseled against a **"closed orthodoxy"** that proponents use to impose their educational views on others (LW 3: 259), claiming that a closed mind and a closed orthodoxy about educational questions mean that different sciences of education "are not only possible but also much needed" (LW 3: 259). Knowing that many think "science by its very nature is a single and universal system of truths," he added that the "idea need not frighten us," because even "in the advanced sciences, like mathematics and physics, advance is made by entertaining different points of view and hypotheses, and working upon different theories" (LW 3: 259).

In order to clarify his fear of dogma that is disguised as science, he added that "there is no one *thing* which is beyond question . . . [and] there is no likelihood that there will be until society and hence schools have reached a dead monotonous uniformity of practice and aim, [and consequently] there cannot be one single science" (LW 3: 259).

Thus, he objected to dogmatism that forbids classroom discussions (LW 14: 234) and pedagogy that always pushes for "a certain view as the correct one" and seeks to "develop closed minds" (LW 9: 160). He warned us that there is "an atmosphere of fundamentalism" in scientific and political thought and that this "atmosphere has penetrated the schools" (LW 9: 162). When pedagogical, scientific, and political fundamentalists invade schools, there is little reason to believe that they will either value reflective educators or reflective students. Even so, the classroom teacher

> has to avoid all dogmatism in instruction, for such a course gradually but surely creates the impression that everything important is already settled and nothing remains to be found out. He has to know how to give information when curiosity has created an appetite that seeks to be fed, and how to abstain from giving information when, because of lack of a questioning attitude, it would be a burden and would dull the sharp edge of the inquiring spirit. (LW 8: 144)

Beyond avoiding dogmatic attitudes and practices, he spoke of the importance of understanding the differences between an education that is suitable for humans and a training that is appropriate for animals (LW 8: 162). He argued that dogmatic instructional attitudes and techniques destroy "the spirit of wonder" in children (LW 8: 143) and asserted that ideas and materials ought to be "supplied by way of stimulus, not with dogmatic finality and rigidity" (LW 8: 324). However, he also recognized that the teacher has to protect "the growing person from those conditions which occasion a mere succession of excitements which have no cumulative effect, and which, therefore, make an individual either a lover of sensations and sensationalism or leave him blasé and uninterested" (LW 8: 144).

Dewey's other concerns about dogma and dogmatic thinkers in the field of education included some that touch the teacher's professional development and the growth of students. He saw intelligence arrested when **indoctrination** was a tool of a dogmatic educator or an educator in a dogma-driven education system. He argued that the resulting indoctrination was not at all education, but "the systematic use of every possible means to impress upon the minds of pupils a particular set of political and economic views to the exclusion of every other" (LW 11: 415).

Indoctrination

instructional approaches that seek to implant beliefs in such a fashion that they will always remain secure, even in the presence of conflicting facts and arguments

He extended his objections to indoctrination as he explained how logic and epistemology entwined with social and political philosophy from two angles: indoctrinating students into a desirable political mindset or into an undesirable political mindset. He rejected the idea of indoctrinating students into a new social or political paradigm, saying, "I do not think that indoctrination regarding a new social order is either desirable or possible. The wisest person in the world does not know what that new order is going to be, and the best way to get ready for it is to take care of the present" (LW 11: 574). Conversely, he added that "schools have been guilty of a great deal of indoctrination . . . in nationalism, miscalled

patriotism. Everybody ought to have public spirit, but the indoctrination of 'patriotism' has given us a narrow, vicious type of nationalism and party strife" (LW 11: 574–575).

In reality, then, the dogmatic elements in education have many causes, manifestations, and consequences. When they arise in professional and institutional settings, the problems are made more challenging when people confuse education with training and indoctrination. The challenge of unveiling pedagogical dogma hiding under the shield of a science of education is also a complicated but necessary endeavor. Dewey suggested a more favorable outcome when he encouraged teachers to nurture reflective students in reflective ways for a reflective society.

A Picture of a Reflective Society

Though Dewey wrote on one occasion of an imaginary utopia that does not have any schools, he would no doubt encourage—at least for the foreseeable future—a society with schools and other educational entities that is ultimately antithetical to the dogmatic teacher, politician, parent, and student. The dogmatic thinker would not be at home in Dewey's ideal society, at least not much of the time. However, what can society do to counter the growth of dogmatic thinkers and to promote the development of reflective thinkers? Actually, society can do a variety of things according to Dewey, although two general options may cover the scope of alternatives. First, Dewey challenged us to develop societies that uniformly promote a growing, thinking populace. Second, he proposed that schools complement the educational thrust of society with a distinct educational mission: the promotion of a growing profession and student population.

Of the many ways Dewey's ideal democratic society can guard itself against the influence of dogma, dogmatic education, and dogmatic thinkers, there is one endeavor that supports and furthers all others, namely, the unending pursuit of new information and understanding. More precisely, he believed that we should encourage new knowledge if for no other reason than to ensure that old knowledge does not become binding and blinding beliefs: "Continued progress in knowledge is the only sure way of protecting old knowledge from degeneration into dogmatic doctrines" (MW 12: 98).

To this specific educational mission, Dewey tied a series of efforts. The pursuit of new information, knowledge, and understanding should occur in every facet of life and institution of society. That is to say, the search for fresh insight and understanding ought to be a regular part of the activities of government agencies, judicial bodies, business entities, civic organizations, religious groups, and educational institutions. If we build this kind of learning, educative society, we will constantly be strengthening the influence of good schools, for "Every place in which men [women, and children] habitually meet, shop, club, factory, saloon, church, political caucus, is perforce a schoolhouse" (MW 7: 304). Good teaching, then, is needed in "doctors' offices, in museums, newspaper plants, farms, forests, steamboats, buses, art studios, factories, stores, government offices, civic concerts, theaters, public discussions, and in the thousand other enterprises of living" (LW 5: 541).

Why, however, was Dewey so adamant about societal agencies and entities becoming effective educational agencies? Clearly, he thought that schools, even if they are doing their best, are no match for the rest of society if it is anti- or miseducative. The weight of society's anti- or miseducative influence can overwhelm teachers and schools, reducing them to shallow centers of socialization. Schools and society, therefore, need to cooperate if we are going to reach the goal of developing a society of reflective people or at least a sufficiently large portion of the populace to sustain and expand a democratic way of life. The connection between democracy and education is also clear: New discoveries, inventions, insights, data, and facts help keep existing knowledge from degenerating and decaying and they nurture a free

and just society. Similarly, they provide new perspectives on old issues, refine merited conclusions, challenge questionable assumptions, complement firm beliefs, destabilize indefensible opinions, expose unethical activities, and support emerging theories.

In "The Intellectualist Criterion for Truth," Dewey reasoned that the "essential difference between truth and dogma" is that truth is "to some extent remade" while dogma is not (MW 4: 74). "Indeed," he continued, "it is only through such application and such remaking that truths retain their freshness and vitality" (MW 4: 74). A glimpse of his notion of truth and knowledge emerges as he asserted, "If we put ourselves in the attitude of a scientific inquirer in asking what is the meaning of truth *per se,* there spring up before us those ideas which are actively employed in the mastery of new fields, in the organization of new materials" (MW 4: 74). What is needed is "the candor, courage and sympathetic insight of minds which move outside any technical fold," minds characterized by "a spirit free from petrification and wooden literalness" (LW 3: 345).

The second way of contributing to the development of a reflective society is by examining the concept of a reflective person and by fostering the qualities of this kind of person in schools. In "The Bearings of Pragmatism upon Education," he explained how his experimentalist view of education could be operationalized. In doing so, he also clarified a crucial difference between the dogmatic and the experimentalist mind:

> Instruction carried on upon this basis would teach the mind that all ideas, truths, theories, etc., are of the nature of *working hypotheses.* One of the chief obstacles to the progress of the race has been the *dogmatic* habit of mind, the belief that some principles and ideas have such a final value and authority that they are to be accepted without question and without revision. The *experimental* habit of mind, that which regards ideas and principles as tentative methods of solving problems and organizing data, is very recent. An education based upon the pragmatic conception would inevitably turn out persons who were alive to the necessity of contin-

ually testing their ideas and beliefs by putting them into practical application, and of revising their beliefs on the basis of the results of such application. (MW 4: 188)

Schools, therefore, should abandon all dogmatic assumptions in favor of "the experimentally tested character of the object known in consequence of reflection" (LW 4: 146). All claims by administrators, teachers, and students then become "hypothetical, non-dogmatic" (MW 7: 144). Understandably, Dewey found it "worth noting that the capacity (1) for regarding objects as mere symbols and (2) for employing symbols instrumentally furnishes the only safeguard against dogmatism, i.e., uncritical acceptance of any suggestion that comes to us vividly; and also that it furnishes the only basis for intelligently controlled experiments" (MW 4: 95). The stimulation, cultivation, and practice of reflection and experimentation, therefore, become important objectives and means for the school and, thereby, for society. In nourishing reflection and experimentation, though, it is important from Dewey's orientation that there be a rejection of "formal logic, with its creed of absolute certitude," for it "abhors the very mention of adventure and risk, the life-blood of actual human thinking, which is aroused by doubts and questions, and proceeds by guesses, hypotheses and experiments, to a decision which is always somewhat arbitrary and subject to the risk of later revision" (MW 7: 133).

Experimental thinker

a person who emphasized the importance of viewing ideas as hypotheses that need to be tested and used in the process of learning

If the development of the reflective and **experimental thinker** is a safeguard against the emergence of the dogmatic thinker, academic freedom becomes a necessary educational condition. He argued that freedom of "mind," "thought," "inquiry," and "discussion, is education, and there is no education, no real education, without these elements of freedom" (LW 5: 332). As a result, we need to recognize that "an attack upon what is called academic freedom is an attack upon intellectual integrity, and hence it is an attack upon the very idea of education and upon the possibility of education realizing its pur-

pose" (LW 5: 332). Thus, the highest praise that can be given to a teacher is that a student had an intellectual awakening, developed the "power to think," and had learned "to face facts and to face them regardless of the consequences" (LW 5: 333). To develop in students "habits of doubt" through study, then, is to be admired, not shunned (LW 6: 272). Or we could say that the development of an experimental attitude is a desired outcome of study and a deterrent to dogmatic thinking (LW 6: 276). Importantly, Dewey believed that the experimental attitude views a generalization differently from the way the non-experimental perspective does, seeing it as an instrument for further inquiry or as "a hypothesis, not a dogma" (LW 7: 343). The implications of these thoughts for the teacher are neither simple nor obvious, but it is clear to Dewey that one pertinent educational goal is the development of "a spirit of curiosity that will keep the student in an attitude of inquiry and of search for new light. If the result is simply to leave the student with the idea that there are two sides to the question and there is a great deal to be said on both sides, the effect may be only a new version of the right answer affair; there are now two sides instead of just one" (LW 9: 180–181).

For Dewey, then, schools and educators in a democracy do have a role in nurturing a democratic environment that leads to intelligence and reflection and a clear toleration for intellectual diversity: "A democratic system of education cannot go the length of prescribing conclusions. It leaves no room for dogmatism in this sense. In the end it must rest its case on faith in intelligence" (LW 11: 559). With this orientation, we are not surprised to learn that Dewey made claims regarding the advantages of a philosophy of education that prizes open, inquiring atmospheres: "They rule out all dogmatism, all cocksureness, all appeal to authority and ultimate first truths; they keep alive the spirit of doubt as the spring of the work of continually renewed inquiry" (LW 11: 484). So, he argued against censorship and for a curriculum and pedagogy that involves "the discussion of a wide variety of opinion, unorthodox and orthodox, with an intelligent teacher in the classroom" (LW 14: 373). A discussion of widely differing orthodox and unorthodox ideas, he felt, is

> the best protection the schools can afford against our students being later misled by unscrupulous propagandists of one doctrine or another. It is surely better for our young people to face controversial issues in the open atmosphere of the schoolroom, than to seek out what is forbidden in some dark, unwholesome corner. No thought is so dangerous as a forbidden thought. (LW 14: 373)

In what may sound like—or even be—a contradiction, Dewey claimed that the *"only ultimate* protection against dogmatism" is a genuinely scientific attitude that displays a willingness to reconsider, to examine alternatives, and to question existing and emerging possibilities (LW 17: 443; emphasis added). This scientific spirit, then, he characterized as a new approach to thinking that has resulted in "new methods of inquiry and reflection [that] have become for the educated man [and woman] today the final arbiter of all questions of fact, existence, and intellectual assent" (LW 9: 22–23). Ultimately, then, Dewey argued that each person must learn to judge matters or come to think for herself although he noted that such language is tautological, for "any thinking is thinking for one's self" (LW 8: 324).

Conclusions

We have reached a point where we may wish to raise questions about and objections to Dewey's descriptions and claims about dogmatic and reflective thinkers. We may query him about, for instance,

1 his explanation of the causation of dogma and dogmatic thinking;
2 the conceptual boundaries of the idea of a dogmatic thinker;
3 the association of nearly the entire universe of negative educational outcomes with dogmatic thinking;

4   his philosophical anthropology in view of his evo-
     lutionary theory of origins;
5   his instructional practices given his pedagogical
     theory.

More importantly, though, we may wish to ask if
Dewey made a dogma out of his view of reflective
thinking. Did his emphasis on the idea lead blindly
to asking questions that minimize and depreciate
intuitions, feelings, and instincts? Did he fail to
question his own beliefs, especially his most prized
ones (LW 8: xvii)? Did he practice a non-dogmatic
form of thinking?

These questions and similar ones were not strange
to Dewey. He acknowledged that he sometimes wrote
in a "somewhat dogmatic shape" because of con-
straints of space and time to qualify his thoughts
(EW 5: 54). Even so, he hoped that the shape of his
discussion did not lead to the conclusion that he
was "dogmatic in spirit" (EW 5: 54). As well, Dewey
made both a spatial and a pedagogical defense of
his perceived dogmatism, claiming: "From limita-
tion of space, I can only state salient points quite dogmatically, and cannot undertake to prove what I
have to say" (EW 5: 413). Dewey also attempted to
disarm his readers when he admitted that he "may
seem dogmatic" about his theory of knowledge at
times but really was not when his views were well
understood (MW 3: 112). He acknowledged too that
he wrote "somewhat dogmatically" when recapitu-
lating his criticism of a position but did so because
he was not making an argument as such for or against
the position: He was merely synthesizing previously
stated objections (MW 13: 51).

Two further points need attention. First, it seems
safe to say that Dewey, as he said of Froebel, expected
those who study his ideas to think for themselves and
use the best available data, evidence, and reasoning
to critique him (MW 1: 84–85). So, even if Dewey was
dogmatic at times, his encouragement of independent, reflective thinkers undermines dogmatic thinking, whether his or another's.

Second, critical insight into Dewey's overall

understanding of the dogmatic thinker is provided by what we term his paradoxical epistemology. While he held that philosophical, political, religious, economic, scientific, and social doctrines and beliefs could and often do influence a person to think and be dogmatic, they need not. The person's attitude toward and the way she or he holds doctrines, assumptions, and opinions are the pivotal considerations. That is, will the person genuinely allow or encourage criticisms by others? Will she stop others from questioning? Does she keep learning, questioning, and considering? Does she keep asking herself uncomfortable questions, such as "Am I as critical of my own beliefs as I am of those who disagree with me?" For these and other reasons, Dewey's epistemological paradox is well summarized in *A Common Faith*. In the same paragraph that he claimed that his faith in the experimental method is unshakable, he said that he was open to accepting new findings and rejecting current beliefs:

> A "creed" founded on this material [the experimental method of intelligence] will change and grow, but it cannot be shaken. What it surrenders it gives up gladly because of new light and not as a reluctant concession. What it adds, it adds because new knowledge gives insight into the conditions that bear upon the formation and execution of our life purposes. (LW 9: 56–57)

Lest we naively accept Dewey's ideal of using a pedagogy of reflection and the goal of fostering reflective students, it is worth pausing to note that there are "vices of reflection" (MW 14: 137). Among the vices that he mentioned are:

1   we may become overly interested in "the delights of reflection";
2   we may develop an anemic or evasive form of thinking;
3   we may become afraid of assuming the responsibilities of decisive choice and action;
4   we may become absorbed in the abstract and avoid pressing realities;
5   we may delude ourselves into thinking we have

a love for truth when we are actually "only indulging a pet occupation" (MW 14: 137).

Added to this list of vices is his conclusion that we may engage in "reflection" so we can further our own biases, defend our prejudices, and escape personal relationships (MW 14: 136–137). Reflection, then, is no panacea. Instead, Dewey both encouraged and cautioned us about what we consider reflection and urged that we not allow distortions of the idea to immobilize or deceive us.

GLOSSARY

Closed orthodoxy—a point of view that is characterized by one's belief that the true way of understanding philosophical, scientific, religious, or educational questions has been achieved *and* that there is no need to be open to revising or rejecting the position in the future.

Dogmatic thinker—a person who feels and thinks that certain assumptions, ideas, and facts are permanently settled and that they do not need to be reconsidered for clarification, revision, or rejection.

Empirical thinker—a person who typically engages in thinking that is based largely on unexamined and unreflective personal experience.

Experimental thinker—a person who emphasizes the importance of viewing ideas as hypotheses that need to be tested and used in the process of learning; an approximate synonym for reflective thinker.

Indoctrination—instructional approaches that seek to implant beliefs in such a fashion that they will always remain secure, even in the presence of conflicting facts and arguments.

Judgment—the activity of deciding which intellectual claims are based upon relevant facts and arguments, the significance of these facts and arguments, and whether other considerations and inquiry are needed before making a decision.

Open-mindedness—an active disposition to listen, learn, and reflect on the ideas, facts, and arguments discussed by others.

Perspectivism—the theory that a person's thinking is either partially or completely determined by her context, experience, and philosophy.

Reflective thinker—a person who is disposed to examine and evaluate the different grounds she and others have for believing and disbelieving truth claims, assumptions, and traditions.

Scientific thinker—a person who emphasizes the importance of studying issues from a scientific or reasoned position; an approximate synonym for reflective thinker.

CHAPTER THREE

The School Curriculum

Although there is a rich tradition of debate about curriculum—its definition, description, design, development, and delivery—in the history of education, extensive discussions have not settled a large number of issues for many, perhaps most, educators much less the general public. Curricular topics remain, therefore, a central point of controversy for educators, policy-makers, and the public for a number of reasons. The grounds for the debate are almost unlimited, including embedded assumptions about the existing views of an educated person, the purposes of schooling, the multiple means to educational ends, the numerous ideals of a particular society, and the agents of selection. Conversely, arguments for different and, sometimes, similar curricula come from people with diverse social and political philosophies, religious beliefs and practices, social and cultural backgrounds, and ethnic and racial heritages. Within these competing and complementary perspectives are emotionally and intellectually charged issues that involve questions regarding professional

autonomy, public input, human nature, intellectual freedom, character development, separation of church and state, political responsibility, respect of persons, and democratic values.

A superficial acquaintance with the aforementioned controversies may lead us to want to walk away in disbelief and disgust, wondering why we cannot argue less, agree more, and get on with educating students. In reality, there probably is more agreement on specific aspects of the **curriculum** than is emphasized by those who engage in curriculum theorizing. However, it would be a mistake to think that consensus is either easy or widespread, except on somewhat tangential and surface matters. Crucial concerns, though, are not far below the surface and are raised on a regular basis by those who are interested in questions of democracy, equity, compassion, justice, freedom, excellence, and respect. Even so, there are other dimensions of the curriculum that are important but not sufficiently valuable to debate seriously, much less divide a school or community. Still other portions of the curriculum are sometimes matters of indifference. Where a curriculum question falls in the realm of the contested, a commonality, or the insignificant will also vary at times from community to community, person to person, and teacher to teacher. Of course, it is important at times to ask why a specific curriculum concern or practice is a dead issue. Should the practice, for instance, be problematized or shown to be an issue? Does the curriculum or practice need to be deconstructed? Are we sleeping on a curriculum bed that is eroding the intellectual development of students and the democratic growth of society?

Dewey stepped into the discussion to ask if our indifference as educators and citizens to certain curricular concerns is partly responsible for student disinterest in learning. If the ideas and experiences of a curriculum are not important enough for us to reflect on and debate, why should our children and students care about them? Moreover, our curricular indifference or lack of valuing certain domains

Curriculum

a term that is variously used to describe a set of learning opportunities, educational materials, or official learning plans

may raise other important questions. For example, do our perspectives on certain curricula indicate that our interpretations of them need to be questioned, that some studies should be purely elective, that the curriculum should be based in part on the interests of students, and that coming to understand and debate controversial issues is more important than an acquaintance with lifeless ideas? In the spirit of a curriculum nonconformist, Dewey complained that adults have created an educational world that has excluded Education herself until students are believed to be ready for her. Sadly, he claimed, adults have intentionally designed schooling in such a way that children are never considered prepared to meet Education. Education is always someone to be met in the future, never in the present. Even so, some people can still converse with Education and may whisper to her:

> Our much preparation is a thick wall
> Through which thy yet continued call
> Arrives suppressed, altered in sense
> We built laborious, learning's fence,
> Behind which we hide from thy creations
> Till we change by safe translations
> Wild things wondrous spoken in a tongue
> Once our own, native, personal; now hung
> Stammering and alien, language
> Of us who labor for scant wage
> In lands where we are foreign born
> Living protected, safe,—and forlorn. (Boydston, 1977, 52–53)

Needless to mention—or almost so—is the conclusion that when we exchange a **wild things curriculum** for *a curriculum of safety and forlornness,* we undermine teaching and learning, educational means and ends, and democratic discussions and goals. Instead of developing students with reflective minds by means of stimulating curricula, we develop pedantic minds where the contents of prefabricated academic rooms are neatly pigeonholed, including the library where the tables

Wild things curriculum

an expression that alludes to the experiences, ideas, and problems that strongly appeal to a student

> Are heaped with engraven labels,
> At second-handed auctions bought,

Of lectures, books and annotations—
Cheap gather'd substitutes for thought—
All sworn affidavits to allege
Such things are just that knowledge
That's fit for wise men in a college. (Boydston, 1977, 78)

Dewey, as we have seen, did not diminish curriculum controversy. Indeed, he added to the debate in order to keep us thinking about important questions, whether obvious or undeveloped. The questions of curriculum, for him, were too important to walk away from, even if they were not easily answered. Immediately, the questions and answers are important, because they influence the enthusiasm of the teacher for teaching and, even more critically, the passion of the student for learning. Transitionally, the issues are important because they affect the means and methods of teaching and learning and whether reflection, experimentation, and discovery will be an important part of classroom activities. Ultimately, they are important because they affect the answers we give to two critical questions: First, what kinds of students do we want to develop in and emerge from schools and, second, what kind of society do we want to prepare students to live in, contribute to, nurture, and shape? Alternatively, in the case of the second question, what kind of society, do we want assisting and complementing schools with their educational responsibilities? Moreover, do we want to cultivate graduates who think for themselves and help build a better society or are we satisfied with people who unthinkingly follow the leadership of the elected, the powerful, and the privileged? As one of many other options, do we want to nurture a few critical thinkers and ethical citizens and a much larger number of largely unreflective consumers and workers?

Dewey's view of the ethics of democracy has significant implications for answering these questions. Consequently, these questions, as well as others, are examined as we investigate his view of the curriculum. Curriculum, of course, can be understood and approached from many angles. Commonly, curriculum may be seen as the plans and materials that a school provides for student learning. Many, though, speak of the intended, learned, and assessed curriculum. Others talk of the overt and covert or hidden curriculum. Still others write about other interpretations of the curriculum, such as the official or explicit, unofficial or implicit, and neglected or null curricula. These and other accounts of the curriculum offer insights and raise issues that are invaluable and should be examined by anyone wishing to obtain an in-depth understanding of curriculum ideologies and issues.

Our approach offers an alternative orientation to curriculum, one that fits with Dewey's ideas although his approach could be treated differently. As we explore his view of the curriculum, we examine what we call

1   the *ecological* or environmental dimensions;
2   the *anthropological* or human dimensions;
3   the *pedagogical* or instructional dimensions;
4   the *epistemological* or knowledge dimensions.

While this interpretative scheme is initially peculiar to those who have pursued more traditional approaches to curriculum studies, it offers the advantage of raising awareness about and pulling together curricular components that are sometimes overlooked. More importantly, the framework offers a useful way of understanding Dewey's thoughts.

We distinguish four curricular dimensions for the convenience of discussion, but they are not separate entities if we follow Dewey's thinking. Indeed, one of Dewey's major curricular emphases was that the curriculum should be understood in terms of its continuity, interaction, and unity because human experience, including the academic, should be characterized by these qualities. Given his emphasis on human experience, it is crucial to understand that the anthropological dimensions permeate all phases of the curriculum. Because education is a set of social experiences, humans—students, teachers, and others—are consistently involved regardless of whether the topic of analysis is the ecological, pedagogical,

Epistemological curriculum

an allusion to traditional school subjects and to the theory of knowledge or grounds for making truth claims in these subjects

or **epistemological curriculum.** Consequently, the four domains overlap, commingle, and blend. He wanted us to understand the importance of this comprehensive view of as well as integrated approach to curriculum so that we will recognize that a curriculum is being delivered and learned regardless of whether we are discussing Nazi Germany, quieting a boisterous clique, making a remark about the brutality of professional boxing, shivering in a cold classroom, observing a religious holiday, treating an obese student sensitively, encouraging a student to analyze a political issue, smelling the odors of the cafeteria, or discussing our summer vacations. The curriculum is, in this sense, whatever is being taught and learned regardless of whether it is official, planned, designed, assessed, covert, overt, and so forth. Our discussion is, therefore, designed to cover what many call both the formal and informal curricula. Dewey referred in part to the latter curriculum as **"collateral learning"** (LW 13: 29). Believing that collateral learning is often more important than the planned lesson because it involves the "formation of enduring attitudes, of likes and dislikes," he concluded that "the greatest of all pedagogical fallacies is the notion that a person learns only the particular thing he is studying at the time" (LW 13: 29). Collateral learning may involve any number of ideas, values, beliefs, and prejudices. If we think collateral learning does not occur, Dewey would describe us as naïve about the nature of schools and the various curricula.

Collateral learning

a reference to the many things students learn that are not a part of the formal and intentional curricula of the teacher or school

As we examine the ecological, anthropological, pedagogical, and epistemological elements of the curriculum, several ideas are worth keeping in mind. First, Dewey himself did not use this terminology to describe his thoughts about the curriculum. We employ it to help capture dimensions and nuances of his thought that are not otherwise readily grasped. Second, our use of the terms is a casual one and not meant to represent the precision that would be used by ecologists, anthropologists, epistemologists, and others. Third, the same curricular experience, subject, or inquiry may fall within more than one

domain, depending on the way it is conceptualized or explained. Consequently, the designations are not ways to pigeonhole different aspects of the curriculum. Instead, they are lenses to wear—and throw away—at times to help us see particular Deweyan emphases. Fourth, it is important to recognize that the title of this chapter—The School Curriculum—is intended to draw attention to learning experiences in the school. But this does not mean that the flow of learning outside of school should not be similarly analyzed. In reality, the **ecological curriculum** outside of school explains, in part, the internal ecological curriculum. However, the two might be largely discrete, antithetical, and fragmented and make the challenges of teachers greater. Finally, like most educational thinkers, Dewey thought that curricular experiences should promote the goals or objectives of the school. Among these goals, of course, is that of cultivating reflective students who are assisted in their pursuit of thinking independently so that they can keep growing and contributing to the **growth** of democratic schools and societies.

Employing the term *curriculum* to cover all of the student's learning experiences is advantageous in several ways but provides no basis for making curricular selection decisions. The criteria for making curricular decisions are somewhat beyond the explicit scope of this work but were explained by Dewey in a variety of publications, including his well-known *Experience and Education* (1938). His ideas regarding educative, noneducative, and miseducative experiences provide a broad framework for thinking about the selection of learning experiences. Reading this brief work, while demanding, is rewarding for those who are enthusiastic about curricular issues.

The Ecological Dimensions

As we use the term *ecology*, it refers to the non-human environmental factors that affect the learning of students, such as the material conditions of neighborhoods, the economic circumstances of fam-

---

Ecological curriculum

a reference to the fact that the constructed and natural material and physical world possesses and communicates significant information and values to students and teachers

---

Growth

a term Dewey used to indicate the worthwhile development of a person in the present that also provided abilities and dispositions for that person to continue developing and contributing to a democratic society

ilies, the physical facilities of schools, the technological resources of classrooms, and the cultures of schools and classrooms. Obviously, the human dimensions of the curriculum cannot be isolated from the ecological, for broadly conceived the ecological includes human interactions as well as our creations and nature. In particular, for Dewey, the educational **environment** was anything, whether present in the school or in the external environment, that impinges upon the thinking and learning of students (Simpson & Jackson, 1997, 119ff.). Strictly speaking, then, there is substantial interpenetration and overlap between the ecological and the anthropological dimensions of the curriculum, because teachers and students are significant entities of the total school environment. In the ecological domain, Dewey is probably best known for his emphasis on the classroom environment or conditions. But he did not ignore the other facets of the environment. His discussion of the world of people and things makes this obvious. To be sure, he compared the broader social environment to classroom conditions so that we can grasp the import of what he was saying:

Environment

a word that refers to the immediate and distant factors that influence a student's feelings and thinking as she learns

> we live from birth to death in a world of persons and things which in large measure is what it is because of what has been done and transmitted from previous human activities. When this fact is ignored, experience is treated as if it were something which goes on exclusively inside an individual's body and mind. It ought not to be necessary to say that experience does not occur in a vacuum. There are sources outside an individual which give rise to experience. It is constantly fed from these springs. No one would question that a child in a slum tenement has a different experience from that of a child in a cultured home; that the country lad has a different kind of experience from the city boy, or a boy on the seashore one different from the lad who is brought up on inland prairies. (LW 13: 22)

We are largely but not exclusively interested in the world of things in this section, but, of course, physical, material, and technological circumstances cannot be separated from people, especially in the live

worlds of communities, schools, and classrooms. The physical or material environment, as Dewey observed, has an impact on people and vice versa. Thus, when speaking of the physical features of the broader environment and aesthetics education, he commented on their impact:

> I do not see how any very high popular artistic standard can exist where a great many of the people are living in slums. Such persons cannot get artistic culture simply by going to free concerts or the Metropolitan Museum to look at pictures, or the public library to read books, as long as their immediate surroundings, or what they come into direct contact with, unconsciously habituates them to ugly, sordid things. A small number of people may come through with genuine aesthetic appreciation even under these circumstances. Even those who have, economically speaking, the most opportunities for higher culture, become insensitive to the ugliness that exists in our human environment. Architectural critics point out, for example, that there are slums on Park Avenue as well as in other quarters of the city. The packing box architecture, produced for the sake of profit, has its advantage over that of tenement houses, but it is hardly of a type to raise the aesthetic and artistic standards. (LW 6: 45)

With his interest in making art and aesthetic experiences a part of everyday life, Dewey had a double concern for students who live in aesthetically offensive neighborhoods—whether in affluent or slum settings—and then spend all of their school days in facilities that are artistic tragedies (LW 10: 346). In all likelihood, students will not come to see or will have great difficulty in understanding that art and aesthetic experiences should be a normal part of living. They will probably think of "art upon a remote pedestal" (LW 10: 24, 11). While it is not the responsibility of most teachers qua teachers to change the artistic qualities of their communities or focus exclusively on the subject of art or even the artistic and the aesthetic elements in the curriculum, Dewey did think one of their major duties is to understand the influence of environmental conditions. He argued that teachers should appreciate, first, the principle of

shaping experience by designing the surrounding environment, second, the importance of selecting environmental conditions that promote growth, and, third, the imperative of extracting the worthwhile from surroundings for educative experiences (LW 13: 22).

Recognizing the influence of the physical, material, and technological environments and their interactions with human environments and utilizing this knowledge to help build educative experiences for students is a necessary but not sufficient step for the teacher. She needs to understand the connections between school and community environments, whether physical, emotional, social, intellectual, or political. She should be "intimately acquainted with the conditions of the local community, physical, historical, economic, occupational, etc., in order to utilize them as educational resources" (LW 13: 23). Dewey believed, then, that if we are going to effectively educate students we need to understand at least three kinds of environments: the classroom, school, and neighborhood. Similarly, he argued that we need to understand the latter in order to design the first two in educative ways.

We have already observed that the educational situation is more complex than having just three environments. The multiple environments that teachers need to understand include those that she helps build and use (the internal environments of the school) and those she ought to understand and utilize to complement and supplement the internal environments (the external environments of the school). Upon reflection, it is easy to conclude that these two kinds of environments have multiple subtypes. For example, *the internal environment* may be approached through the lenses of *classroom* environments, including the human or anthropological dimensions of tutorial, individual, small-group, and full-class environments. The classroom environments are influenced by the availability of relevant educational materials and technology and the changing of these elements. Each time a set of materials, equipment, resources, Web sites, so forth is

updated, added, or changed the classroom environment changes. The internal environment also has *school* environments that can be analyzed by different cultures, functions, and space into smaller environments, e.g., cafeteria, gymnasium, chemistry laboratory, library, restroom, corridor, and computer laboratory. These are the environments that the teacher needs both to help build and use in the educational process. While her primary responsibility is to develop her classroom environments, she has a duty to work with other teachers, administrators, and volunteers to build other school environments that will complement one another for the education of students.

Similarly, *the external environment* may be seen through the eyes of a close neighborhood association, broader community, nearby parks, close businesses, underground subways, retail malls, and other entities. Hence, the environment "is whatever conditions interact with personal needs, desires, purposes, and capacities to create the experience which is had" (LW 13: 25). As a result, we can see that the ecological and the anthropological dimensions of the curriculum blend together and include the educator's activities, the educational materials, and the social setting or interactions within the environment. The emotional and academic ethos that is created is also important. Specifically, "what is done by the educator and the way in which it is done, not only words spoken but the tone of voice in which they are spoken" convey a message (LW 13: 26). The ecological setting includes "equipment, books, apparatus, toys, games played. It includes the materials with which an individual interacts, and, most important of all, the total social set-up of the situations in which a person is engaged" (LW 13: 26). Intriguingly, Dewey said that the social relationships or anthropological dimensions of the curriculum are the "most important of all" (LW 13: 26). We will, of course, return to this topic later and explore why Dewey drew this conclusion.

Given this understanding, there are not only

multiple environments that influence the student but also multiple dimensions of each environment that affect learning. The dynamic nature of these environments and their dimensions is another key consideration. As the student passes from one place, role, group, or teacher to another, different experiences, situations, and opportunities become available. Seeing the connection of one environment to another is facilitated as the student moves in and out of them, for "as an individual passes from one situation to another, his world, his environment, expands or contracts. He does not find himself living in another world but in a different part or aspect of one and the same world" (LW 13: 26). What the person learns in "one situation becomes an instrument of understanding and dealing effectively with the situations which follow. The process goes on as long as life and learning continue" (LW 13: 26). Building environments, of course, is more than an individual teacher's responsibility, for no one person can build or sustain multiple environments by herself. If teachers work together, the challenge is to arrange environments and experiences that form desirable kinds of behaviors and habits. Specifically, it is to

> secure that organization of equipment and facilities which will give the children typical and varied contacts with the materials of experience, so arranged as to further consecutive and orderly growth. What the school can supply which the informal life of the home and the neighborhood lack is arrangement of materials and modes of action; such an arrangement that the information which is of most value shall be gained while the trivial is eliminated; such that there shall be constant growth of insight into the principles which underlie experiences; and that there shall be increasing command of methods of work—of inquiry, discussion, and reflection. The school building is treated not as a collection of rooms in which lessons are learned and recited, but as a well-equipped and organized environment for carrying on certain modes of work, and thus securing certain experiences and the formation of certain habits. (MW 1: 335–336)

Many schools and classrooms, obviously, are not reflectively planned, aesthetically appealing, instructionally adaptable or, even, emotionally welcoming. So they are counterproductive when it comes to facilitating the work of the teacher. Instead, the physical facilities teach mixed or, worse, counterproductive messages. Because many schools are underfunded and neglected, their materials are limited, their equipment is antiquated, their organization is hierarchical, and their activities are prescribed, they may communicate a variety of negative lessons, e.g., education is a low priority, students are not highly valued, teachers can work in any circumstances, and democracy is for adults. From a socioeconomic and political frame of reference, these schools may teach that the children of the working class and/or poor are not as important or as valued as the children of the middle and wealthy classes. Schools that are adequately funded and maintained get across a different set of lessons.

When schools as a whole, including teachers and students, work to create desirable kinds of environments with sufficient funds, students are much more likely to grow and their environments will be more prone to widen and deepen. So, as the environment expands, students come into "connection with new objects and events which call out new powers, while the exercise of these powers refines and enlarges the content" of experience (LW 13: 49). In the process, the teacher utilizes "subject-matter found in the present life-experience of the learner" or uses "existing experience as the means of carrying learners on to a wider, more refined, and better organized environing world, physical and human, than is found in the experiences from which educative growth sets out" (LW 13: 55). The teacher, then, has to "find ways for doing consciously and deliberately what 'nature' accomplishes in the earlier years" (LW 13: 49). In a sense, the teacher has to become more effective than "nature" because what children and youths naturally learn may be noneducative or miseducative as well as educative. Her focus is tapered as she seeks

to develop educative, growth-producing, and enhancing experiences. The wise teacher, therefore, uses the prior experiences of students as an invaluable aspect of an educative set of curricular experiences.

In educative school and classroom environments, Dewey believed that genuine problems of students—problems that emerge from their psychological development, present lives, social learning, and classroom engagements—should be common classroom or school stimuli. However, he said that it is not uncommon to see the inquisitive child before school turn into a passive one in school. In fact, he largely—and, perhaps, simplistically—blamed teachers and schools for creating passive students. Only genuine problems, in his estimate, can help reverse the tendency to cultivate passivity, for no

> improvement in the personal technique of the instructor will wholly remedy this state of things. There must be more actual material, more stuff, more appliances, and more opportunities for doing things, before the gap can be overcome. And where children are engaged in doing things and in discussing what arises in the course of their doing, it is found, even with comparatively indifferent modes of instruction, that children's inquiries are spontaneous and numerous, and the proposals of solution advanced, varied, and ingenious. (MW 9: 162)

School conditions, however, are often not sufficiently oriented around authentic student problems, critical reflection, and educative experiences: "They are much better adapted to the acquisition of a body of fixed information than to investigating operations of inference, discovery, and proving" (MW 6: 455–456).

The teacher's challenge is twofold and both aspects of the problem need to be addressed in part by the teacher becoming or remaining a student, a permanent learner. The teacher as student takes several forms, two of which demand attention. First, the teacher needs to study the distinct qualities, interests, dispositions, habits, and thinking of each student so that she understands the curriculum—or

ideas, values, and cultures—each student brings and adds to the classroom environment. Second, the teacher needs to understand "[1] the conditions that modify for better or worse the directions in which individual powers habitually express themselves" and recognize [2] that educational methodology "covers not only what [she] . . . intentionally devises and employs" but also "the atmosphere . . . of the school which reacts in any way upon the curiosity, the responsiveness, and the orderly activity of children" (MW 6: 217). Understanding that the environment of the school is one form of educational methodology illustrates how the ecological and the pedagogical dimensions of the curriculum merge at times.

Other dimensions of the conditions of the school and the classroom are too numerous to list much less discuss, but several should be identified. The arrangement of furniture, the structure of buildings, the type of furnishings, the lighting in classrooms, and the availability of technology, to mention but a few items, all help create an ethos that is educationally productive or counterproductive. The interactions among students, the decisions regarding students, the flow of classroom visitors, and the role of administrators in daily affairs contribute negatively and positively to conditions. Every activity, event, entity, or factor that cultivates conditions which promote a maturing, holistic experience for students is important. Indeed,

> anything that breaks the latter [environment] up into fractions, into isolated parts, must have the same influence [of fragmentation] upon the educative growth of the child. It may, however, be admitted [by some] that these conditions, while highly important as regards the aims of education, have little or nothing to do with the course of study—with the subject-matter of instruction. But a little reflection will show that the material of study is profoundly affected. The conditions which compel the children to be dealt with en masse, which compel them to be led in flocks, if not in hordes, make it necessary to give the stress of attention to those studies in which some sort of definite result can be most

successfully attained, without much appeal to indi-
vidual initiative, judgment or inquiry. (MW 1: 269)

Environmental conditions—the ecological curriculum—can overpower the formal subject matter
or epistemological curriculum, then, in at least two
ways. First, they can be so powerful that they virtu-
ally replace or seriously impair students' engage-
ment in learning specific subjects. The focus turns
from the learning of literacy skills or science to the
uncomfortable temperature, the roaches scurrying
around, the acting out of students, the poor lighting, the interruptions for announcements, the noise
of trucks emptying dumpsters, or a myriad of other
factors. Second, conditions—especially the number
of students or the number of students with pro-
nounced learning, emotional, and behavioral challenges—may become the determinants of curriculum
in unfortunate ways. That is, the environment,
including students, determines which studies will
be explored or stressed because there is a need to
have a measurable outcome demonstrated (MW 1:
269). The traditions and policies of a school and
district—the broader educational environment—
intrude into the classroom to have similar effects. The
explicit curriculum learned in these situations may
then become that "individual initiative, judgment
or inquiry" do not really matter. The real curriculum
is learning how to score well on achievement tests.
Reflective thinking is not tested and will be more or
less neglected or ignored (MW 1: 269).

In closing our discussion on this general theme,
we move to Dewey's view of how the structure and
organization of schools and the nature of curriculum
design become a part of the classroom curriculum.
In a sobering statement, Dewey claimed that single-
grade teaching assignments, isolated grade levels,
and single-subject teaching responsibilities help
build a school environment that *undermines* the
complete development of students and the effectiveness of teachers:

Unless the teacher has opportunity and occasion
to study the educative process as a whole . . . , it

is impossible to see how he can deal effectively
with the problem of the complete development
of the child. The restriction of outlook to one limited year of the child's growth will inevitably tend
in one of two directions: either the teacher's work
becomes mechanical, because practically limited to
covering the work assigned for the year, irrespec-
tive of its nutritive value in the child's growth; or
else local and transitory phases of the child's development are seized upon—phases which too often
go by the name of the interests of the child—and
these are exaggerated out of all due bounds. (MW
1: 270)

Consequently, Dewey believed that we should not
waste the knowledge that teachers have of students.
Nor should we design school structures that impede
learning. Instead, we should understand that:

It is easy to fall into the habit of regarding the
mechanics of school organization and administration as something comparatively external and
indifferent to educational purposes and ideals. We
think the grouping of children in classes, the
arrangement of grades, the machinery by which the
course of study is made and laid down, the method
by which it is carried into effect, the system of
selecting teachers and of assigning them to their
work, of paying and promoting them, as in a way
matters of mere practical convenience and expediency. We forget that it is precisely such things as
these that really control the whole system even
on its distinctly educational side. No matter what
is the accepted precept and theory, no matter what
the legislation of the school board or the mandate
of the school superintendent, the reality of education is found in the personal and face-to-face contact of teacher and child. The conditions that
underlie and regulate this contact dominate the educational situation. (MW 1: 267–270)

Matters of "practical convenience and expediency"
(MW 1: 267)—the hallowed havens of educational
bureaucrats—need to be examined to determine
their negative and positive influences on teachers and
students. The negative qualities need to be altered
and the positive supported.

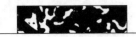

The Anthropological Dimensions

As we employ the phrase *anthropological dimensions of the curriculum,* it refers to all of the human interactions that students experience in school. Broadly conceived, however, Dewey thought that the external **anthropological curriculum** may enter the classroom via the memories, feelings, and thoughts of each student and can be more influential than the internal human curriculum. Understanding each child helps the teacher identify and utilize the external and internal anthropological curricula. Within the school environments and interactions of teachers, students, administrators, staff, volunteers, and parents, we find this extremely powerful element of the curriculum. While anyone who comes into contact with a student is a potential part of her anthropological curriculum, we will focus primarily on the probable anthropological curriculum at school, curricular elements that are drastically underestimated by many curriculum designers and developers.

Dewey thought the two most important kinds of anthropological curricula are the student and the teacher. More precisely, he said the "personal contact of child with child, and of children with teacher" is where we find "the reality of education" (MW 1: 268). He added, "In this contact, and in it alone, can the reality of current education be got at. To get away from it is to be ignorant and to deceive ourselves. It is in this contact that the real course of study, whatever be laid down on paper [in the official curriculum], is actually found" (MW 1: 268). While recognizing that policy makers, administrators, and supervisors help establish policies and practices and other conditions that support or inhibit the work of the teacher and the learning of students from one another, Dewey stressed that "the real course of study" (MW 1: 268) comes through personal contact between students with students and students with teachers. The "lively give-and-take of ideas, experiences, information, between members of the class" are invaluable elements of the curriculum (LW 8: 329). What influenced him to draw this conclusion?

Anthropological curriculum

a reference to the fact that students and teachers and others in schools and communities possess significant bodies of understanding and ways of thinking that influence learning

Dewey's conclusion has several explanations, but one of the most important rationales is seeing students as curricula. Students bring with them to school several curricula—their cultures, beliefs, languages, and values as well as their understanding of life, science, religion, and social problems—that ought not to be ignored in effective classrooms. Instead, they need to be utilized in educative learning experiences. Among other curricula, Dewey stressed that students offer one another the opportunities to learn about and enjoy different cultures, languages, religions, races, abilities, perceptions, and values (MW 9: 14ff). The wealth of information that students bring to class is unsurpassed in relevancy and potency for their classmates or peers. Seeing the student as an important facet of the anthropological curriculum also opens another curricular window: The individual student can obtain a better understanding of her own heritage, strengths, and perceptions. Utilizing the resources of student experience and knowledge enables the teacher to more readily and steadily ensure that the course of study is indeed a *course:* "it ought to be a flowing, moving thing, for its subject matter comes into continuous contact with the minds of the pupils" (MW15: 183).

A second reason why Dewey emphasized the importance of the human curriculum inside the school is that he thought that "the real course of study [in the school] must come to the child from the teacher" (MW 1: 273). This is true, he believed, because what the student learns is largely dependent on the teacher's preparation, alertness, reflection, and dispositions. Indeed, she communicates what she understands and thinks about educational materials, subject matter, social concerns, and other students to each student. Her understanding—whether deep or shallow, reflective or dogmatic, sensitive or calloused—often becomes the understanding of students (MW 1: 273–274). His emphasis on the thorough preparation of the teacher in her teaching fields, of course, does not undermine the importance of teaching materials, software, books, and other educational apparatuses. In fact, it underlines

the importance of intelligently prepared educators selecting and using the best materials and equipment. These materials should help the teacher as she assists in making learning experiences "vital, adequate, and comprehensive" rather than "mechanical, superficial, and restricted" (MW 1: 273–274). He clarified his notion of the teacher as curriculum when he claimed that she may either be a dry, dull fact or an exciting, living spirit:

> There is no way by which subject matter, as laid out by experts, can get over to the pupils, except through the medium of the teacher. We can have a text-book written in accordance with the recommendation of experts. But after all, will not the last thing that counts be how the teacher uses that text-book; how it is handled; the questions that are asked? You can have very rich, full subject matter laid down on paper, and yet the personality and intelligence of the teacher may be such that the subject matter will shrink, dry up, and become a mere trickle of dull fact when it gets to the pupil. You can have an outline of a course of study, in the form of a bare skeleton on paper, and yet that course of study, as it gets over to the pupils in the classroom, may be very full, rich and alive, because of the spirit that the teacher puts into it; the methods the teacher uses; the assignment of outside study that the teacher gives, and new points of view in the student mind. (MW 15: 183–184)

Think for a moment about what Dewey said: the spirit, methods, assignments, and viewpoints of the teacher are critically important in getting the student to learn. To be exact, if the teacher is stale and dry, the skills, ideas, and materials are likely to be the same. If she is intellectually and emotionally alive, the other dimensions of the curriculum are apt to be likewise.

Obviously, many other important curricular elements are the secretaries, student interns, volunteers, custodians, cafeteria personnel, guardians, coaches, school nurses, parents, counselors, assistant principals, and principals. What they say and imply and how they behave and think influences students in vital but often imperceptible ways. To underestimate their value is to misunderstand that "face-to-face" interactions overshadow policies, plans, and places. Even so, this is no reason to ignore or devalue these matters, and there is no viable reason to ignore the curricula of the family, neighborhood, community, or society, but these topics are beyond our present focus. However, in a democratic society that seeks to be educative, they cannot be ignored and represent part of the interests of teachers as citizens.

In addition, there are the human curricula that come from the diverse students we have in our classes. Diversity, at the moment, refers to the frequently neglected, often hidden, but powerful experiences and realities of students. Specifically, we are including students who are ostracized and marginalized for reasons of language, ethnicity, race, challenge, religion, or gender. Beyond the students we legally, logically, and ethically identify as being underserved and neglected, there are other students we overlook because they fall below our ethical and legal radar. These students—for instance, the obese, gay, shy, anorexic, abused, homeless, hyperactive, inarticulate, lonely, immigrant, and unattractive—are too frequently neglected or discarded by guardians, parents, peers, and society. Sadly, these same students fare little or no better in many schools than they do outside of school. In Dewey's anthropological curriculum, they are an important part of the lessons we teach about respect, tolerance, equality, fairness, acceptance, and democracy. These students, too, offer curricular options that open doors to the discerning teacher and open doors to democratic or moral education that extend beyond the usual ones. From Dewey's point of view, if everyone is to be equally respected because she or he is a person, the school and the classroom offer places where we can both study and practice our democratic ideals for all peoples.

The Pedagogical Dimensions

As the term *pedagogical* is used in this context, it refers to all of the procedural and methodological aspects of teaching and learning, including but not

limited to full class activities, small group arrangements, and individual inquiry. In Dewey's mind, the conception also includes the dimensions of the classroom and school that are often labeled *climate* and *culture,* e.g., the classroom atmosphere or ethos that is created by the philosophy and personality of school personnel and students. In particular, the pedagogical dimensions of the curriculum become obvious when the instructional methods used and the school culture established get across lessons, albeit often hidden ones, about specific skills, values, and beliefs. The "collateral learning" that is derived from these lessons may be much more important than we understand and either complement or weaken our consciously intended lessons (LW 13: 29). If, therefore, we wish to have a reasonably consistent and coherent curriculum, we can hardly fail to address its pedagogical dimensions.

A look at Dewey's ideas about grouping students is one of the clearest examples of how the methods of education and the school and classroom cultures are an element of the curriculum. Of course, Dewey did not discuss grouping in the light of current research on the subject, but he did raise questions that enable us to understand why there is a pedagogical dimension to the curriculum and how his educational theory values this curriculum too.

When he examined social and educational problems, he was inclined to ask a pointed question: To what ends or for what purposes do we want to group students? Grouping, for example, is frequently believed to allow teachers to focus on the instructional needs of academically similar children and to meet their academic interests more efficiently. In particular, ability grouping is at times said to facilitate teaching similarly developed students specific skills, information, and ideas that are necessary to do well on standardized tests or criterion- or performance-based measurements. On other occasions, emphasis is placed on students learning desirable social behaviors and attitudes. On still other occasions, group activities may be stressed because particular studies

suggest that certain kinds of grouping, e.g., cooperative learning activities, are more efficient and effective than individual activities in furthering certain learning outcomes.

In considering the broader ramifications of this issue, it is worth remembering that Dewey's set of ends or goals is radically different in many ways from that of most present-day politicians and policy-makers as well as those of many educators and parents. Moreover, his perspective is much more comprehensive and holistic than many educational theorists. In addition to being interested in grouping because students constitute a part of the anthropological curriculum, he is interested because he believed

1   education is a social process;
2   the social process of education should be a democratic one;
3   democratic schools should be viewed as community groups;
4   school classes ought to be understood as **social groups;**
5   tension in social groups or classes is a means to intellectual and moral growth;
6   placement of students in groups has the potential to develop collaborative working attitudes and abilities;
7   multi-age level groups enhance the learning and thinking of everyone involved.

Social group

a phrase that indicates we should view students in schools and classes as groups where ordinary interactions lead to worthwhile experiences and learning

To begin with, then, Dewey believed that education is fundamentally a social experience, not a discrete, isolated academic or individualistic one. Education in schools is an adventure that demands an interaction among students and teachers who, in his words, constitute a "social group" (MW 9: 368). He noted that we would be better off if we stopped thinking of the school as a place separated from life and consider it "a miniature social group" where learning and growing are ordinary features of "shared experience" (MW 9: 368). His rationale is simple: Social interactions "involve intercourse, communication, and cooperation" (MW 9: 368). Because of his political philosophy, Dewey envisioned the school

as a community characterized by democratic ideals, procedures, and practices or as a community in which democracy is studied, taught, learned, and lived. As far as he was concerned, the greater the permeation of democratic ideals, structures, and activities in the school and the classroom, the better. Even so, his distinct conception of social democracy needs to be understood, for it illuminates the kind of school and class community he wanted.

> A democracy is . . . primarily a mode of associated living, of conjoint communicated experience. The extension in space of the number of individuals who participate in an interest so that each has to refer his own action to that of others, and to consider the action of others to give point and direction to his own, is equivalent to the breaking down of those barriers of class, race, and national territory which kept men from perceiving the full import of their activity. (MW 9: 93)

In the democratic community group known as a school, Dewey visualized other, smaller social groups of pupils and teachers, not mere collections of people or classes, as are often found in traditional educational institutions. He was interested in the school as a community group and the class as a social group or a set of social groups because these units are indirect and direct means of teaching, learning, and practicing democracy as well as special agents of teaching other kinds of skills and competencies, such as reading, writing, computing, and thinking. The communities or groups are deemed both influential means of teaching and learning specific subjects and significant lessons themselves about democracy and related values.

As we might expect, Dewey argued that diversity in a democratic school is educationally vital. He held that school communities or learning environments should be designed to enable students to escape the parochialism of their own social backgrounds. We might be tempted to think that he only referred to students who come from backgrounds where economic resources are limited. But he did not. Unlike many thinkers, he believed that *all* social

environments or all children's backgrounds are lim-
iting and, therefore, somewhat provincial. To vary-
ing degrees, everyone's environment is inescapably
and unavoidably circumscribed. No familial or cultural background can contain all the riches of the peoples of a society. Facilitating the sharing of experiences
of people from different sociopolitical, cultural, religious, racial, and economic backgrounds is, therefore,
educationally invaluable. To believe that some students have nothing valuable to share with others is
both to misunderstand how much each student
understands and brings to school and to perpetuate
an educational and social parochialism that hand-
icaps the broadening of minds and the development
of democratic ideals. School communities and their
various social groups, therefore, should "see to it
that each individual gets an opportunity to escape
from the limitations of the social group in which
he was born, and to come into living contact with
a broader environment" (MW 9: 24–25). In the
process, students should never be treated as mere
means to desirable intellectual outcomes. They are
to be respected as persons although valued too for
their knowledge, understanding, and cultures.

Dewey was interested in more than a pedagogy
of escape, however. He maintained that the process
of escaping provincialism via diversity is—or at least
should be—simultaneously an entrance into a new,
broader, and liberating environment or environments. His pedagogy of escape, then, is also a pedagogy of liberation, because it is a pedagogy of a
new creation: "The intermingling in the school of
youth of different races, differing religions, and
unlike customs creates for all a new and broader
environment" (MW 9: 26). This creation of broader
learning environments, then, is both an educational
end and a pedagogical means to more growth-
enhancing experiences for everyone, students and
teachers alike.

Dewey's interest in school diversity, therefore, is
in part because he saw it as an indispensable means
of each person's escaping the limitations of her or his

past and entering into a broader and growth-producing present and future. Groups, for him, were a necessary means of learning about diverse experiences and cultures, practicing democratic living, and developing the personal abilities of individuals. Moreover, he assumed that learning and practicing democracy and enjoying personal growth lead people to see that they already have many commonalities as well as enable them to develop additional common concerns. However, people in settings that are based upon social interactions need to keep in mind that common values emerge through an equable interaction with diverse ideas and people:

> There must be a large variety of shared undertakings and experiences. Otherwise, the influences which educate some into masters, educate others into slaves. And the experience of each party loses in meaning, when the free interchange of varying modes of life-experience is arrested. A separation into a privileged and a subject-class prevents social endosmosis. The evils thereby affecting the superior class are less material and less perceptible, but equally real. Their culture tends to be sterile, to be turned back to feed on itself; their art becomes a showy display and artificial; their wealth luxurious; their knowledge over-specialized; their manners fastidious rather than humane. (MW 9: 90)

Briefly stated, a few people—regardless of their economic, educational, political, religious, or racial backgrounds—should not dominate community groups or subgroups in or outside of schools. Diverse opinions and voices ought to be elicited and nurtured if schools and society are to be democratic, educative, and liberating for all if Dewey is correct.

A somewhat parenthetical notion needs attention. Dewey's theory of democracy and understanding of societal pressures influenced him to warn of the potential negative aspects of groups on the individual. He asserted that "the comparative helplessness of persons in their strictly singular capacities to influence the course of events expresses itself in formation of combinations in order to secure protection from too destructive impact of impersonal forces" (LW 13: 108). In context, Dewey went on to discuss "combinations," such as unions, that provide some protection for the individual but which may also inhibit reflection. If we extrapolate from his warning about outright pressuring or subtly socializing people to conform in groups, it is safe to say that community groups (schools) and social groups (classes) have the opportunity to be exploitative and coercive, intentionally and otherwise. So, if schools are to be genuinely democratic and help individuals as well as groups be both strong and healthy, they must be structured, designed, and operated in ways that avoid open and covert manipulation.

In view of this caution, diversity of race, religion, language, ideology, and custom may go beyond providing opportunities for escaping from provincialism and offering occasions to create a broader learning environment. The broader environment that emerges should not aim at a homogenized intellectual or cultural outcome either within groups or across them. The resulting broader environment should enrich warranted or justifiable differences, not extinguish them. Diversity brings "novelty, and novelty means challenge to thought," not a predictable, dead, monotonous perspective for everyone or for subgroups (MW 9: 90). Interpreted in this fashion, challenge of our thinking is unusually consequential for Dewey, for it is essential to the cultivation of reflective thinkers. The absence of intellectual diversity and, thereby, challenging ideas and practices is likely to nurture if not result in stagnant, dogmatic attitudes toward life and learning. Seeing issues from different viewpoints, on the other hand, does not necessarily mean that one opinion is as good as another. Some opinions on certain topics may be equally warranted or similarly unwarranted. In other situations, particular opinions may be warranted and others may not be. However, seeing questions and issues from different perspectives ought not to lead to either-or thinking. Instead, seeing multiple points of view should result in a deeper, more comprehensive and synoptic understanding. As Dewey stated,

"One cannot climb a number of different mountains simultaneously, but the views had when different mountains are ascended supplement one another: they do not set up incompatible, competing worlds" (MW 9: 117). The individual, therefore, needs to broaden or add to her perspectives by seeking additional opportunities to learn and understand.

Conversely, it is clear that people do or will not always see what others see from the same mountain or mountains. Negotiating these discussions is also fruitful from Dewey's perspective. He was aware that when people from different backgrounds start interacting there is increased likelihood of disagreement, tension, and conflict. Disagreement and tension are not necessarily undesirable, however. Rather than shunning tension, he thought that it should be welcomed and allowed to lead to more learning and a greater appreciation of differences. However, if tension is to be productive, schools must be places where students respect one another and learn "good manners," especially the virtues of "politeness and courtesy." As old-fashioned as this idea seems, it was not naively held by Dewey. He knew that manners differ in cultures and countries. Even so, he argued that some "code of manners" is found in all cultures, and it is at least a lubricant that arrests or lessens friction (LW 13: 37). In a society of many cultures, manners become more, not less, important. Accordingly, it is important—if we want to communicate, learn, and have creditability with one another—that we seek to understand and show respect for differences, including customs, manners, and ways of thinking.

If Dewey's reasoning is sound, diverse learning groups are vehicles for learning different and overlapping manners that will enable people to better manifest respect for and work with one another. Rather than ridiculing or ignoring differences, people learn to understand and respect and, ideally, appreciate many differences. Although learning to honor the manners of other peoples is a part of moral education because such indicates respect for them, Dewey insisted that a direct approach to moral education is largely ineffective. Instead, it is "the surrounding atmosphere and spirit" that constitute "the chief agent in forming manners" and other morals (MW 9:22). Once again, educators in schools and classes are primarily responsible for creating a learning atmosphere that will enhance the learning of manners and other morals throughout the various curricula.

So for Dewey, the learning of manners was more than a means of reducing friction and enhancing students' understanding and appreciation of diversity. For him, the lack of manners represented "a failure of education, a failure to learn one of the most important lessons of life, that of mutual accommodation and adaptation" (LW 13:38). If children and youths do not learn to accommodate and adapt to one another, we can hardly expect adults to work together toward common goals. In *Schools of Tomorrow*, Dewey specifically wrote that the **"hardest lesson"** a person has to learn is the "problem of adjustment with his neighbors and his job" (MW 8: 253). He was firmly convinced that "the ability of people to work together successfully" is critical to a healthy community and society (MW 8: 314). Grouping, therefore, is a natural educational means of learning to disagree, argue, accommodate, adapt, adjust, and work with others. To view it as merely a substantively neutral pedagogical technique, therefore, is to misunderstand the critical curricular function it plays.

Earlier we noted that Dewey maintained that each person should have an equitable opportunity to both receive and contribute to discussions in her social group or groups at school. He added that if learning environments influence students and teachers to work and learn together, then future learning will spring from "easy and ready contact and communication with others" (LW 13: 38). This assumption presupposes that schools have helped to develop different kinds of communication "that are inherently appropriate to social situations" (LW 13: 37). Since such

Hardest lesson
a term used to refer to the challenge to live, learn, and work with others in democratic and productive ways

interaction does not automatically occur, schools should cultivate "free and equitable intercourse" (MW 9:90). Here Dewey insinuated that lifelong learning is in part tied to one's ability to talk, collaborate, and work with others.

One final idea about grouping needs attention. Ideally, Dewey wanted several age groups in schools—or **"assembly places"** as he later called them—to draw upon the resources of older students and the expertise of parents, visitors, guardians, and teachers (LW 9: 136). He wanted teachers to direct and guide the learning activities of social groups (classes) in assembly places (schools) with the assistance of selected adults and older students. He particularly mentioned having thirteen- to eighteen-year-olds "who are especially fond of younger children" working with and guiding them (LW 9: 137). Consistent with contemporary thinking, he affirmed the idea that guiding and working with others are natural ways to improve one's own skills and knowledge. Similarly, he felt comfortable encouraging the use of parental expertise in schools. In his view of grouping, then, the presence of people of different age levels adds to a school's diversity and richness.

Dewey seemed both reflective and flexible on grouping questions, but this does not mean that he found any type of arrangement in schools and classes acceptable. Nor would he think that every ethically acceptable grouping is necessarily pedagogically acceptable. For example, certain kinds of groups may have equitable outcomes without stimulating the educative experiences that Dewey's philosophy entails. Equity in the opportunity to receive a poor quality of education or inferior schooling is at most a hollow victory. Dewey insisted on groupings that led to both personal and social growth in a democratically structured and equitably functioning learning community. Contrary to the thinking of some, his interest in using social processes, communities, and groups to enable the learning of democratic ideas and practices, diverse ways of living and thinking, and collaborative means of growing intellectu-

Assembly place

a term Dewey used to suggest that the school should be a place where educators and students assemble before exploring the school and the community for learning opportunities ally and morally was not in opposition to being interested in more narrowly defined achievement outcomes in reading, science, or mathematics. Stating that Dewey was interested in these subjects and disciplines, however, should not influence us to undervalue what students learn about democratic living, common values, reflective thinking, collaborative interaction, mutual accommodation, personal adaptation, social adjustment, free discourse, multicultural sensitivity, and cross-cultural courtesy. Subjects and values are all important in his theory of curriculum.

As a result of his political philosophy, Dewey painted an expansive picture, one that gives a richer, more comprehensive, complex, and complicated context for making judgments about grouping than many provide. Thus, the ethics of grouping was at least as important an issue to him as the science of grouping or the effectiveness and efficiency of grouping. Certainly, any kind of grouping that leads to undesirable outcomes or consequences, for nearly all students would be strongly resisted by Dewey. If it leads to undesirable outcomes only for the children of the poor and powerless and desirable outcomes for the children of the economically advantaged, he would urge us to probe deeper to find ways to avoid practices that advantage the advantaged and disadvantage the disadvantaged. And if grouping resulted in undesirable outcomes for the advantaged but not for the disadvantaged, he would encourage us to use our imagination to plan better for all children. We might also hear him use the word *experiment.*

Dewey was also uncomfortable with any recommendation based upon the belief that we can solve *permanently* our challenge to use groups ethically and efficiently, even if the plan claimed to promote successfully democratic sympathies, collaborative abilities, cultural diversity, reflective thinking, moral discretion, scientific understanding, mathematical facility, technological sophistication, historical perspective, and aesthetic judgment by both individuals and society. Nevertheless, he applauded those who accept and pursue this challenge with the under-

standing that it is an unending task of thinking, discovery, rethinking, planning, researching, and so forth ad infinitum. Finally, he urged us, as we establish policy, organize schools, design curricula, plan experiences, and interact with students, to think as a good and wise community: "What the best and wisest parent wants for his own child, that must the community want for all of its children" (MW 1:5). Grouping, then, is just one example of how a method of instruction may intrinsically involve its own curriculum, lessons, and outcomes.

The Epistemological Dimensions

As we employ the words *epistemological dimensions of the curriculum,* they refer to the courses that are often taught in schools or that frequently constitute the planned or official school curriculum, such as history, art, biology, mathematics, physical education, theatre, chemistry, literature, music, social studies, and physics. Dewey threw into the mix other activities and subjects, such as cooking, sewing, and gardening as well as philosophy, ethics, and psychology. Of course, language studies, e.g., literacy studies and other languages are important, too. Historically, the term *epistemology* refers to a person's theory of knowledge or knowing and involves questions about the criteria for knowledge or truth claims. By implication, we are associating the epistemological dimensions of the curriculum with issues of knowledge and knowing. For example, part of studying history involves understanding the competing theories of historical inquiry and interpretation that lead to different claims and explanations by historians. Examining these competing interpretations enables the teacher and student to more fully understand both the hidden and the explicit curriculum—and the hidden and explicit truth claims of one another. In this section, we examine Dewey's ideas about the planned curriculum from two angles: (1) the curriculum as a set of adult understandings and (2) the curriculum as a set of temporal relationships. In the next chapter, we will examine his view of knowledge or truth

and how it relates to the school curriculum.

As we begin this analysis of Dewey's view of the curriculum as a set of adult understandings, it is obvious that he thought that, at least in part, the curriculum—as both methods of inquiry and bodies of knowledge—included both "the child's present experience" and "the subject-matter of studies" (MW 2: 278). The former aspect of the curriculum underlines the student's understanding and interpretation of the world, and the latter refers to the more developed understanding of adults that is involved in formal inquiry. However, he said more on the topic, emphasizing the importance of "the attitudes, the motives, and the interests" involved in knowledge development (MW 2: 278) and the significance of the intended outcome of the maturing, developing **"adult mind"** (MW 2: 279). What is the value—and how do we use—the curriculum, especially "the adult mind" or "organized bodies of truth," since they are not the child's present mind (MW 2: 278–279)? We use the adult mind in at least three ways, Dewey replied. To begin with, the adult mind provides an end or goal toward which we educate (MW 2: 279). The adult mind, in its somewhat ideal form, serves as a goal for students, educators, and schools. Second, bodies of knowledge help us understand or interpret the child's life and mind and, thereby, provide better guidance for her (MW 2: 279). As the child manifests interests and interacts with the materials and people in her environment, her level and way of understanding suggest where the teacher can begin to assist her as she learns the formal curriculum. Finally, the teacher's grasp of the forms of inquiry and creativity enables her to develop environments that promote the child's growth and utilization of the knowledge she already possesses (MW 2: 291). From this viewpoint, adult knowledge constitutes the construction materials for building educative environments that foster the growth of the student as she develops an enriched and reflective mind.

The adult mind—as it is represented in the thinking of the teacher—provides two benefits. First, it pro-

Adult mind

a mind that is reasonably well informed and has reflective tendencies

vides a means of interpreting the child's existing interests and informs the teacher's pursuit of educational goals. We gain help in understanding that some inclinations of the student are "waning," others are "culminating," and still others are "dawning" (MW 2: 279–280). But these tendencies, impulses, or interests are not determinative in making curricular decisions for the student. They can be for the child's ill or good. They can be educationally helpful or of little or no educational promise. Neither "continuous initiation" of studies fueled by the student's impulses nor "continual repression" of tendencies by the teacher, therefore, is educationally well advised (MW 2:279–280). Second, Dewey concluded that his theory provides a way of evaluating—not just understanding—the child's tendencies, impulses, and interests and provides insight into how they might be used to further develop the child's understanding. He explained: "the subject-matter of science and history and art serves to reveal the real child to us. We do not know the meaning either of his tendencies or of his performances excepting as we take them as germinating seed, or opening bud, of some fruit to be borne" (MW 2: 281).

The significance in the child's experiences and activities, therefore, is that they indicate present and emerging inclinations and abilities. Subject matter is used to interpret these tendencies and abilities and to see how their potential may grow into fuller, richer understanding. Subject matter can then be used to direct or guide the student's growth. Such guidance, however, is not an "external imposition" but *"freeing the life-process for its own most adequate fulfillment"* (MW 2: 281). However, this does not mean leaving the student entirely to herself (MW 2: 281). If we leave the student completely to her interests, independent thinking will be impossible for no one can "evolve a universe out of his own mind" (MW 2: 282). Dewey elaborated on the need for and the nature of direction and its connection to developing the adult mind:

> Development does not mean just getting something out of the mind. It is a development of expe-

rience and into experience that is really wanted. And this is impossible save as just that educative medium [stimulus] is provided which will enable the powers and interests that have been selected as valuable to function. They must operate, and how they operate will depend almost entirely upon stimuli which surround them and the material upon which they exercise themselves. The problem of direction is thus the problem of selecting appropriate stimuli for instincts and impulses which it is desired to employ in the gaining of new experience. What new experiences are desirable, and thus what stimuli are needed, it is impossible to tell except as there is some comprehension of the development which is aimed at; except, in a word, as the adult knowledge is drawn upon as revealing the possible career open to the child. (MW 2: 282–283)

The teacher's duty, therefore, is to see that the logical dimensions of the curriculum are "*psychologized;* turned over, translated into the immediate and individual experiencing within which it has its origin and significance" (MW 2: 285). Therefore, the teacher is concerned with the subject matter

. . . as *representing a given stage and phase of the development of experience.* His problem is that of inducing a vital and personal experiencing. Hence, what concerns him, as a teacher, is the ways in which that subject may become a part of experience; what there is in the child's present that is usable with reference to it; how such elements are to be used; how his own knowledge of the subject-matter may assist in interpreting the child's needs and doings, and determine the medium in which the child should be placed in order that his growth may be properly directed. He is concerned, not with the subject-matter as such, but with the subject-matter as a related factor in a total and growing experience. (MW 2: 285–286)

Growth, however, is not simply change, but change in a worthwhile or positive direction. A significant problem, therefore, faces the teacher who seeks to direct a student's learning: How can the teacher avoid curricular imposition if she needs to select growth-producing experiences that lead to an adult mind? Dewey offered an alternative to imposition, namely, getting the student to become *an insider* to

knowledge: "The legitimate way out is to transform the material; to psychologize it—that is, once more, to take it and to develop it within the range and scope of the child's life" (MW 2: 290). This idea takes us back to Dewey's third point about the use of the curriculum or the organized, logical adult mind. He wrote:

> Now, the value of the formulated wealth of knowledge that makes up the course of study is that it may enable *the educator to determine the environment of the child,* and thus by indirection to direct. Its primary value, its primary indication, is for the teacher, not for the child. It says to the teacher: Such and such are the capacities, the fulfillments, in truth and beauty and behavior, open to these children. Now see to it that day by day the conditions are such that their own activities move inevitably in this direction, toward such culmination of themselves. (MW 2: 291)

Thus, the teacher is to *direct indirectly*—so as not to impose adult forms of knowledge and her interpretation of them on children—the present "powers," "capacities," and "attitudes" of students until they are "asserted, exercised, and realized" (MW 2: 291). In order to do this, we must rely upon "the teacher [who] knows, knows wisely and thoroughly" the realms of understanding and creativity which are a part of what is called the curriculum, for understanding it is essential to understanding both the child's present development and her desirable future development (MW 2: 291).

Previously, we observed that we will examine Dewey's ideas about the planned curriculum from two angles: (1) the curriculum as a set of adult understandings and (2) the curriculum as a set of temporal relationships. This second way of understanding school studies—the curriculum as a set of temporal relationships—now draws our attention. *Temporal,* as presently employed, refers to the importance of the past, present, and future in Dewey's curriculum theory. By *relationships,* we mean all the interactions and associations that human beings have had and are having with one another and with the world.

On the surface, this topic may appear irrelevant to teachers, but Dewey saw it as a critical issue in being able to develop the adult mind while utilizing the existing understanding of the student.

The triadic time consideration—past, present, and future—focuses on the importance of the present in the school curriculum. Dewey's statements about the past, present, and future are related primarily to what he termed the school or education's purpose. Within this framework of purpose, his first explicit statement about the present and future fell in the rather narrow context of a discussion regarding the student's abilities and inclinations. Regarding the future, he asserted:

> With the advent of democracy and modern industrial conditions, it is impossible to foretell definitely just what civilization will be twenty years from now. Hence it is impossible to prepare the child for any precise set of [future] conditions. To prepare him for the future life means to give him command of himself; it means so to train him that he will have full and ready use of all his capacities; that his eye and ear and hand may be tools ready to command, that his judgment may be capable of grasping the conditions under which it has to work, and the executive forces be trained to act economically and efficiently. (EW 5: 86)

In this excerpt, Dewey's beliefs unfold in noteworthy ways, indicating his thinking about how freedom or democracy makes, first, predicting the future more difficult, second, preparing a student for the future more challenging, and, third, rethinking what it means to prepare a student for the future more essential. The third point—rethinking the preparation of the students for the future—he claimed, indicates that we should focus on two matters: Who the student will become as her intellectual, aesthetic, preferential, evaluative, and volitional abilities are cultivated and how she will gain control of her potentialities and powers. Becoming a particular kind of person involves gaining control of one's potentialities in the present, growing in the present, and planning to keep growing in the future. Preparation for the future, then, is developing the over-

all person or student in the present. Education, therefore, "is a process of living [and learning in the present] and not a preparation for future living" (EW 5: 87). "The school," consequently, "must represent present life—life as real and vital to the child as that which carries on in the home, in the neighborhood, or on the playground" (EW 5: 87). If education, instead, focuses on preparing students for a "remote future" that is foreign to the life of the child at home and in her community, it is destined for failure (EW 5: 88).

The psychological side of the child and curriculum, as briefly noted above, is one important dimension of curricular thinking, but there are others. Two of the most important additional dimensions of thinking are seeing the student as a social being and understanding the logical features of the curriculum. Thus, the school's plan to direct and facilitate a student's growth so that she will live in the present and realize her greatest potentialities in the present and the future should include approaching the student's "social activities" through the vehicles of science, literature, history, geography, and so forth. This step is critical because the child needs to be seen from her social side as well as psychological side (EW 5: 85). In particular, the study of content has educative value when it involves seeing these subjects as records of humanity's social lives and progress. As the various subjects illuminate the present through making clear prior struggles and successes, the student develops her understanding and abilities in the present through a study of the past and present. The past—whether history, biology, literature, music, or other subjects—should provide both "social motive and end" and knowledge, skills, and dispositions for controlling one's self and growing in the present and future (EW 5: 90). The psychological and social sides of education, then, are related to one another and come together as the whole student is understood and educated. Indeed, Dewey asserted:

> I believe that the individual who is to be educated
> is a social individual and that society is an organic
> union of individuals. If we eliminate the social

factor from the child we are left only with an abstraction; if we eliminate the individual factor from society, we are left only with an inert and lifeless mass. Education, therefore, must begin with a psychological insight into the child's [present] capacities, interests, and habits. It must be controlled at every point by reference to these same considerations. These powers, interests, and habits must be continually interpreted—we must know what they mean. They must be translated into terms of their social equivalents—into terms of what they are capable of in the way of social service. (EW 5: 86)

For Dewey, then, the relationship of the past, present, and future is not completely a question of one's view of the curriculum. It is also a question of one's view of the student and her development. The idea of developmentally appropriate curricular experiences was not a foreign one for him and should be based in part on understanding social circumstances, student propensities, and future potentialities (EW 5: 85).

Dewey's example of the explorer and traveler in *The Child and the Curriculum* (1902) illuminates his view of the logical dimensions of the curriculum as well as his view of the past, present, and future. In context, he distinguished the logical and psychological aspects of experience and the curriculum. Claiming that the two are interdependent, he asserted that the finished map that emerges from the explorer's notes "orders" and "connects" experiences, but that they are no substitute for the personal experience of the traveler (MW 2: 284). Explicitly, he stated:

Through the map, a summary, an arranged and orderly view of previous experiences [in the past], serves as a guide [in the present] to future experience; it gives direction; it facilitates control; it economizes effort, preventing useless wandering, and pointing out the paths which lead most quickly and most certainly to a desired result. Through the map every new traveler may get for his own journey the benefits of the results of others' explorations without the waste of energy which he himself would be obliged to repeat were it not for just the assistance of the objective and generalized record of their performances. (MW 2: 284)

With implications for the informal and formal curriculum, he added:

> There is, then, nothing final about a logical rendering of experience. Its value is not contained in itself; its significance is that of standpoint, outlook, method. It intervenes between the more casual, tentative, and round-about experiences of the past, and more controlled and orderly experiences of the future. It gives past experience in that net form which renders it most available and most significant, most fecund for future experience. The abstractions, generalizations, and classifications which it introduces all have prospective meaning. (MW 2, 284–285)

While the implications of these ideas for curriculum are numerous, only one will be noted. To begin with, it is interesting to observe that Dewey thought the logical order of curriculum studies is not final and its value is not in the orderliness per se. The potential availability, significance, fruitfulness, and meaning of the studies for students in the present and future are the more important considerations. The logical order is to enable the individual to gain more out of her present and future experience, not serve as a sterile substitute for them. If a particular logical order is counterproductive to enhancing the experience of the individual, it is failing to serve its appropriate role. So, it seems fitting to say that Dewey thought that if the logical order of the curriculum hinders the development of the student it needs to be re-conceptualized so that it does facilitate growth. Specifically, a logically ordered curriculum needs to be psychologized if it fails the tests of availability, significance, fruitfulness, and meaningfulness for students (MW 2: 285). Consequently, these four criteria for curriculum selection and development deepen and go beyond the criterion that learning experiences should be educative, not miseducative or noneducative.

Dewey's view of teaching history also provides insight into how he believed we should connect the past, present, and future. Intriguingly, he opened the door to studying history through the eyes of various peoples. First, he implied that if history is "just the record of the past," it should play a minor role in the curriculum of the elementary school (MW 1: 104). Second, he believed that if history is seen as "an account of the forces and forms of social life" that "the distinction of past and present is indifferent" (MW 1: 104), for the two commingle. He instantly amplified his thoughts by alluding to the moral value of examining social life: "Whether it [social life] was lived just here or just there is a matter of slight moment. It is life for all that; it shows the motives which draw men together and push them apart, and depicts what is desirable and what is hurtful" (MW 1: 104). So, he said of the study of history, "Whatever history may be for the scientific historian, for the educator it must be an indirect sociology—a study of society which lays bare its process of becoming and its modes of organization" (MW 1: 104). If children of diverse backgrounds are to learn about those things that "draw men [and women] together and push them apart," it seems highly inappropriate to ignore their own histories and experiences and, at the same time, highly appropriate to have them study their own sociologies (MW 1: 104).

Beyond these thoughts, Dewey moved on to a variety of other curricular questions and issues. In his discussions, he was invariably arguing for a wild things curriculum instead of a curriculum of safety and forlornness (Boydston, 1977, 52–53). Among other ideas, his ongoing philosophizing about a wild things curriculum entailed at least two responsibilities. First, that the problems used to stimulate learning and thinking should emerge from the lives of students (the anthropological curriculum). Second, the presentation of problems **(the pedagogical curriculum)** ought to be sufficiently compelling to arouse students to look for facts and information and lead them to new problems (the epistemological curriculum). The teacher's design of the educational environment (the ecological curriculum) is a crucial step in promoting and directing student learning. Problem-centered learning, then, becomes an ongoing process or "a continual spiral" (LW 13:

Pedagogical curriculum

a phrase that indicates that methodological and procedural choices in teaching convey explicit and implicit lessons to students

53). The spiral of curriculum planning, environment construction, problem solving, and student learning is one that is a joint process that engages students and educators, not just curriculum planners in district or government offices. Without this local and personal involvement by students and teachers, our schools are doomed to stale worksheets, discussions, lectures, books, and programs or cheap "substitutes for thought" (Boydston, 1977, 78).

Conclusion

The ecological, anthropological, pedagogical, and epistemological dimensions of the curriculum, as Dewey saw them, all merge together in the school and society. The various curricula, however, are not necessarily consistent in their emphases and values. They may voice different, complementary, competing, and conflicting ideas as the student's mind is developed. This dynamic exists between the four curricula in the school as well as between the school and societal curricula, which turns out to be both unfortunate and fortunate. Obviously, miseducative elements can and do undermine the educative ones at times. At other times, though, the clashing curricula can produce a disequilibrium that provokes questioning and problem solving. This happy outcome, for Dewey, occurs infrequently for many students. At least, the disequilibrium is too often settled without adequate reflection. A person who is unprepared to think reflectively tends to make wild conjectures (LW 8: 202). These guesses may occur in schools as much as they do outside if a student is inexperienced in solving problems or addressing conflicting ideas.

In contrast, if the curricula are reasonably coherent and educative at school, the development of adult minds—minds informed by facts and ideas and formed with reflective tendencies—is expedited. Teachers and others are able to prepare students for the future by fostering their present abilities through a carefully designed curriculum, including the ecological, anthropological, pedagogical, and epistemological dimensions. They foster reflection by and on the curricula as they enable students to draw on the past and address genuine current problems. They realize that the relevant past is important because thinking involves looking "back over what has been done so as to extract the net meanings which are the capital stock for intelligent dealing with further experiences" (LW 13: 59). The problems that arise and are used by teachers are not simply assigned tasks, however. School and classroom environments or situations are problematic only if they arouse perplexity, puzzlement, confusion, or bewilderment. Otherwise so-called problems are artificial, mere exercises that do not promote growth (LW 8: 201), because growth "depends upon the presence of difficulty to be overcome by the exercise of intelligence" (LW 13: 57).

Dewey's problem-and-reflection oriented curriculum theory places great demands on teachers. As implied above, they are responsible for attending to two matters that promote immediate and future learning. First, they are responsible for ensuring that educative problems are situated in the life of the student. Second, they are obligated to plan experiences so that they lead from one challenging problem to another (LW 13: 53). This twofold challenge will be too demanding if only the school-based epistemological curriculum is considered. When educators recognize, however, that the external environment and curricula enter the school each morning with students, they can use them to design the school curricula and to enhance student learning. They can also use them to pursue school curricular goals. In all of their curricular work, however, teachers need to recognize that probably "the most frequent cause of failure in school to secure genuine thinking from students" is "the failure to insure the existence of an experienced situation of such a nature as to call out thinking in the way in which . . . *out-of-school situations do*" (LW 8: 194; italics added). New in-school learning needs to draw, build, and reflect the actual problems and challenges students face in their everyday lives. To ignore the natural connections of the school curricula to life curricula

is to ignore the natural learning opportunities that are related to personal and social concerns, matters that make a difference in ordinary living and growing.

GLOSSARY

Adult mind—a mind that is reasonably well informed and has reflective tendencies.

Anthropological curriculum—a reference to the fact that students and teachers and others in schools and communities possess significant bodies of understanding and ways of thinking that influence learning.

Assembly place—a term Dewey used to suggest that the school should be a place where educators and students assemble before exploring the immediate (school) and extended (community) environments for learning opportunities.

Collateral learning—a reference to the many things students learn that are not a part of the formal and intentional curricula of the teacher or school.

Curriculum—a term that is variously used to describe a set of learning opportunities, educational materials, or official learning plans.

Ecological curriculum—a reference to the fact that the constructed and natural material and physical world possesses and communicates significant information and values to students and teachers.

Environment—a word that refers to the immediate and distant factors that influence a student's feelings and thinking as she learns.

Epistemological curriculum—an allusion to traditional school subjects (e.g., history, biology) and to the theory of knowledge or grounds for making truth claims in these subjects.

Growth—a term used by Dewey to indicate the worthwhile development of a person in the present but which also provided abilities and dispositions to students to continue developing and contributing in the future to a democratic society.

Hardest lesson—a term that is used to refer to the challenge to live, learn, and work with others in democratic and productive ways.

Pedagogical curriculum—a phrase that indicates that methodological and procedural choices in teaching convey explicit and implicit lessons to students.

Social group—a phrase that indicates we should view students in schools and classes as groups where ordinary interactions lead to worthwhile experiences and learning.

Wild things curriculum—an expression that alludes to the experiences, ideas, and problems that strongly appeal to a student.

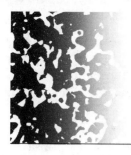

CHAPTER FOUR

The Democratic School

In this chapter, we describe Dewey's supposed beliefs about how a democratic school must ensure, among other matters, that students openly debate and then vote to decide who should serve on the school board, which candidate should be selected as district superintendent, who should be appointed as school principal, which applicants should be offered teaching contracts, what school and subject goals and objectives are acceptable, what district and school budget items will be approved and funded, which subjects should be included in the curriculum, how long the school year should extend, which foods ought to be served in the cafeteria, which sports will be financially supported and offered, who deserves to be retained and promoted each year, and when schools ought to be consolidated and closed.

Actually, Dewey's concept of a democratic school is slightly—or should we say *radically?*—different from the scenario described above. The state of affairs described above is far from his philosophy of a democratic school. To begin, he did not think that the

philosophy and values of a democratic school are primarily marked by students' voices alone. Educators, legislators, and the public have voices, too, and not all decisions in a democratic school—or society— should be determined by a majority vote. Responsible voting is important, but it is only one factor among many others in a school that seeks to understand and practice democratic ideals and professional responsibility in an educative environment. Professional and legal responsibility for the operation of schools ought not to fall primarily on students but on educators and elected representatives. In his opinion, then, schools are not places where majority opinion prescribes the details of policy, employment, practice, and curricula.

In order to obtain a better picture of Dewey's democratic theory and philosophy of education, we will explore five domains. First, we seek to understand his conception of democracy and determine what it emphasizes. Second, we explore his idea of education and its relationship to schooling. Third, we investigate the theory of **knowledge** he believed supports a democratic philosophy of life and education. Fourth, we survey the theory of ethics that he thought stimulates and sustains democratic ideals. Fifth, we look—but throughout rather than as a discrete topic— at how these various elements (democracy, education, knowledge, and ethics) clarify the roles, responsibilities, goals, and activities of a school. From time to time, all five of these themes blend together as they form an integrated philosophical gestalt. Exploring these realms will also indicate just how cranky Dewey was when it comes to critiquing public schools.

Knowledge

a common term that often implies that we have convincing reasons and evidence for being absolutely sure that a statement or proposition is true, but for Dewey it meant that we have cogent grounds for making a provisional truth claim

A Conception of Democracy

Democracy for Dewey was a complex set of relationships that has at least three major emphases and a number of sub-themes. The three general emphases of democracy are the political, the social, and the individual. They are also referred to by Dewey as democracy as a form of government (LW 11: 236), an associated way of living (LW 13: 155), and a personal way of life (LW 14: 226). The interdependence of the political, social, and individual or personal dimensions of democracy is obvious. Isolating one element of democracy from the other two would ultimately destroy it if Dewey's understanding is accurate. So individual, social, and political democratic ideals and practices are interwoven in his theory, and no one of the three can survive or be healthy without the other two. Even so, the themes may be distinguished for discussion purposes.

Political Democracy

Political democracy
a phrase that alludes to a form or structure of government that is based on the values of freedom, equality, opportunity, tolerance, justice, openness, and participation

For Dewey, **political democracy**, the "structure of a self-governing society" (LW 14: 224), included both positive and negative freedoms, freedom for certain kinds of beliefs and actions and freedoms from particular restrictions and boundaries. Positively, freedom for belief and action includes, among other matters, civil liberties and guarantees of "free inquiry, free assembly and free communication" as well as "the right to equal opportunity" in order to develop one's gifts (LW 14: 226–227). Negatively, democracy in its governmental form should provide, again among other things, freedom from "intolerance, abuse, calling of names because of differences of opinion about religion or politics or business, as well as because of differences of race, color, wealth or degree of culture" and "sex, birth, and family" (LW 14: 227, 226). More generally, political democracy joins social and **personal democracy** to nurture freedom and protect people "from coercion and imposition by others" so that each person can "lead his own life" (LW 14: 227).

Personal democracy
a reference to a person being so characterized by democratic attitudes, dispositions, habits, and behaviors that her character is formed by them

Dewey tied together the ethical, legal, administrative, and egalitarian elements of political democracy. Indeed, he went beyond these implications to argue that democracy as a form of government ensures that the voices and votes of everyone count as interests, policies, and participation are considered, encouraged, and realized. Democracy is, he argued, "a form of government which does not esteem the well-being of one individual or class above that of

another; a system of laws and administration which ranks the happiness and interests of all as upon the same plane, and before whose law and administration all individuals are alike, or equal" (MW 10: 137–138). "But," he quickly concluded, "experience has shown that such a state of affairs is not realizable save where all interests have an opportunity to be heard, to make themselves felt, to take a hand in shaping policies. Consequently, universal suffrage, direct participation in choices of rulers, is an essential part of political democracy" (MW 10: 137–138).

An ethical element carries democratic practice in government, communities, and schools still farther. For instance, the ethical is obvious in fostering a concern for equal respect, personal freedom, mutual interests, and voluntary responsibilities. More precisely, he claimed, "democracy inevitably carries with it increased respect for the individual as an individual, greater opportunity for freedom, independence and initiative in conduct and thought, and correspondingly increased demand for fraternal regard and for self-imposed and voluntarily borne responsibilities" (MW 6: 418). Various countries, he believed, at different times have made progress toward democratic ideals, but no nation he felt had yet fully realized these goals. Indeed, a complete, final realization of a democracy seems impossible since we are continually in the process of debating, clarifying, and refining it (LW 11: 299).

Dewey also recognized that political democracy is related to other matters, including economic and industrial circumstances. He thought, for example, political democracy—official or legally recognized freedom, justice, and equality—without economic resources for everyone results in undemocratic realities, and he maintained that the accumulation of wealth by a few and the condition of poverty by many "makes the task of democracy constantly more difficult" (MW 8: 404). The more economic resources that rest in the hands of a minority the less likely the rights, interests, and needs of the majority will be protected. Moreover, he warned of the danger of busi-

ness leaders damaging both democracy and education by too single- and narrow-mindedly pursuing profits (MW 8: 402). The dangers of a business-dominated democracy include turning a genuine democracy into a bourgeois democracy, a democracy where in practice the franchise is limited because "power rests finally in the hands of finance capitalism, no matter what claims are made for government of, by, and for all people" (LW 11: 296). When a bourgeois democracy is established and expanded, authentic democracy is undermined and eroded. If the negative influences of "economic forces" are ignored, Dewey thought we would run the risk of "brutal and unjust **consequences"** (LW 8: 85). For these reasons, it is critical to understand that democracy is never automatic or guaranteed and must be fostered throughout a country.

Thus, a morally responsible political democracy needs to ensure that the antagonism or tension between business's pursuit of profit, an individual's enjoyment of freedom, and society's common good is understood and balanced (LW 7: 349). This task is never permanently settled, for times, circumstances, and people change. Political democracy at all levels, therefore, needs to address issues of corporate power, individual wealth, personal poverty, private freedom, and common good. To ignore these tensions in a professed democracy is to set the stage for a functionally—regardless of the official declarations and professions—undemocratic society and, thereby, open the door to a transformation into an authoritarian form of government that protects the privileges of the powerful, wealthy or not. A totalitarian government, however, is inconsistent with democracy, for it violates its basic principle: *"the ends of freedom and individuality for all can be attained only by means that accord with those ends"* (LW 11: 298).

Consequences

a word that refers to the outcomes of feeling, thinking, and behaving in particular ways that are important in determining their value or worth in school and society

Social Democracy

A political democracy—while historically it may not come first and may only be enshrined in order to protect other democratic values—is important

because it provides a formal constitutional, legal, and structural framework or foundation that enhances the opportunity for further kinds of democracy. By itself, however, political democracy is inadequate, as Dewey's discussions of power and wealth suggested. Actually, political democracy is unlikely to exist by itself (except in the case of a deteriorating democracy), for it does not easily arise without a sufficient base in social and individual democratic sympathies and practices. Of **social democracy** or democracy as a way of associated living, Dewey argued that it goes far beyond governmental matters to encompass everyday affairs and involves living, learning, and thinking with others. It involves communicating with one another, developing shared interests, and breaking through barriers of misunderstanding. Thus, he claimed that democracy is much more than a way of governing and is principally, in his thinking, a way of "living, of conjoint communicated experience" (MW 9: 93). Specifically, it involves each person taking into consideration the interests and actions of others as we make plans for our own lives and, thereby, the "breaking down of those barriers of class, race, and national territory which [keep] . . . men [and women] from perceiving the full import of their activity" (MW 9: 93). Living that is characterized by democratic interactions, regard for others, and shared communications needs to permeate, first, social activities and, thereby, governmental thinking and actions.

Dewey, nevertheless, said more about the primacy of associated living, claiming that when democracy is carefully examined it cannot be sustained politically unless it is also complemented by a social democracy with a clear moral vision and at least a fourfold focus:

> A social democracy signifies, most obviously, a state of social life [1] where there is a wide and varied distribution of opportunities; [2] where there is social mobility or scope for change of position and station; [3] where there is free circulation of experiences and ideas, making for a wide recognition of common interests and purposes, and [4]

Social democracy

a way of living that is characterized by the enactment of the values of a political democracy and is noted for its common interests, social interactions, and open communication

> where utility of social and political organization to its members is so obvious as to enlist their warm and constant support in its behalf. (MW 10: 138)

These four elements—opportunities are numerous, varied, and open to all; mobility is genuine and ongoing; sharing multiple experiences, ideas, and interests leads to common concerns; and social and political organizations and opportunities are, and are seen to be, truly open, accessible, and valuable to all—are crucial aspects of a social democracy. Only if equal opportunity is genuine, mobility is authentic, common interests are realized, and organizations and resources are accessible in everyday activities, has social democracy become the engine that motivates both democratic political structures and personal dispositions. A social democracy, then, involves the everyday and continuous voices of people for freedom, justice, equity, respect, fairness, concern, and opportunity for all. Without these forceful voices, political democracy becomes open to economic, class, race, gender, religious, and ideological values and practices that are antithetical to a true democracy.

Dewey's rationale for this fourfold focus was explicit and included the need to avoid the development of layers of classes and the fossilization of society as well as the need to promote shared interests and experiences:

> Without ease in change, society gets stratified into classes, and these classes prevent anything like fair and even distribution of opportunity for all. The stratified classes become fossilized, and a feudal society comes into existence. Accident, rather than capacity and training, determines career, reward, and repute. Since democracies forbid, by their very nature, highly centralized governments working by coercion, they depend upon shared interests and experiences for their unity, and upon personal appreciation of the value of institutions for stability and defense. (MW 10: 138)

Dewey pressed democracy's moral connection further by arguing that there is an educational connection between freedom of the mind and political

and social freedoms. Our "democracy," he maintained, "is not yet conscious of the ethical principle upon which it rests—the responsibility and freedom of mind in discovery and proof" (MW 3: 230). In order to create and sustain these and related ethical, educational, political, and social responsibilities, then, democracy must be cultivated on an ongoing basis, not ignored as if it has a life of its own and will flourish without attention. He stated that education is a critical feature in a democracy and maintained that the emotional and intellectual qualities associated with democratic ideals must be intentionally cultivated.

Since a moral democracy and the qualities needed to support such do not grow spontaneously "on bushes," they have to be planted and nurtured. They are dependent upon education.

> It is no accident that all democracies have put a high estimate upon education; that schooling has been their first care and enduring charge. Only through education can equality of opportunity be anything more than a phrase. Accidental inequalities of birth, wealth, and learning are always tending to restrict the opportunities of some as compared with those of others. Only free and continued education can counteract those forces which are always at work to restore, in however changed a form, feudal oligarchy. (MW 10: 138–139)

In order to avoid "accidental inequalities" and being ruled by a few or a financial or bourgeois democracy—which in reality is an oligarchy—Dewey pulled together the responsibilities of governmental, economic, religious, cultural, and social institutions into the moral mission of democracy as he set forth the criterion of **growth** by which to evaluate them: "Government, business, art, religion, all social institutions have a meaning, a purpose. That purpose is to set free and to develop the capacities of human individuals without respect to race, sex, class or economic status" (MW 12: 186). To emphasize his thought, he added, "Democracy has many meanings, but if it has a moral meaning, it is found in resolving that the supreme test of all political institutions

Growth
the concept that the development of a person's dispositions and habits of thinking and acting is intrinsically worthwhile and contributes in the present and the future to personal and social development

and industrial arrangements shall be the contribution they make to the all-around growth of every member of society" (MW 12: 186).

Finally, Dewey stated that the cause of democracy is the same as the cause of "the dignity and the worth of the individual" (LW 13:303). He asserted that the underlying values of democracy provide us with an opportunity to experiment or to see if we are going to profitably and helpfully learn together. Indeed, working toward respect, toleration, and interaction and exploring different means to become more democratic are critical, for they are the only means by which we can carry out "the greatest experiment of humanity—that of living together in ways in which the life of each of us is at once profitable in the deepest sense of the word, profitable to himself and helpful in the building up of the individuality of others" (LW 13: 303). This experiment, though, may fail. Actually, it does fail on an episodic basis, but it need not fail continually and ultimately. If democracy moves from the legal and legislative halls of society and into associated ways of living, it has the opportunity to be successful. However, a part of the meaning of living with others in democratically profitable ways is to practice personally the democratic values we profess.

Personal Democracy

We may wonder how the political and social dimensions of democracy are sustained and expanded. Does democracy expand and perpetuate "itself automatically" as long as citizens are "reasonably faithful in performing political duties" (LW 14: 225)? While political duties are necessary ingredients in the survival and expansion of democratic principles, Dewey believed that they are not sufficient and cannot ensure our ideals will be realized. Will these ideals be automatically assured by democratic ways of associated living in neighborhoods, communities, and cities? While democratic living in communities is crucial to a healthy democracy, it too is insufficient alone or even in combination with the

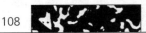

existence of political democracy. In actual fact, Dewey believed we have to keep recreating democracy by "deliberate and determined endeavor" or "conscious and resolute effort" (LW 14: 225, 224) because our political and social democracies are insufficient by themselves.

The significance of the personal and individual nature of democracy becomes apparent here. We need to support, sustain, and spread political and social democracy by developing and living personal democracy. As Dewey said, we need a democracy that "signifies the possession and continual use of certain attitudes, forming personal character and determining desire and purpose in all the relations of life." (LW 14: 226) Ultimately, this means that we cannot overcome the enemies of democracy unless we create "personal attitudes in individual human beings" and abandon our tendency to believe that democracy's defense is found in external structures and forces, e.g., "military or civil" (LW 14: 226). Instead, we need to develop a democracy that is embedded in "individual attitudes" and "personal character" (LW 14: 226).

Surprisingly, but perhaps not, Dewey took a step beyond the need for each person to develop democratic attitudes, qualities, dispositions, and habits. These democratic possessions—attitudes, qualities, dispositions, and habits—are definitely necessary, but they are just as certainly insufficient. They are means to be nourished and need an underpinning that supports and promotes them. For him, a personal faith in democracy is the foundation of these tendencies and behaviors and of a democratic spirit. Only a personal faith in the potential of democracy and human nature can sustain and enhance these possessions or qualities. This personal faith enables a person to call on and use democratic and educative means even when she or he is tempted to resort to authoritarian and propagandizing measures to reach defensible ends or goals. Democracy is a personal way of life that is "controlled by a working faith in the possibilities of human nature. Belief in the

Common Man [and Woman] is a familiar article in the democratic creed. That belief is without basis and significance save as it means faith in the potentialities of human nature as that nature is exhibited in every human being" (LW 14: 226).

A democratic personal way of life is in part dependent upon social circumstances and controlled by "faith in the capacity of human beings for intelligent judgment and action if proper conditions are furnished" (LW 14: 227). To those who object to the need for this personal faith in the potential of human nature and intelligence, he asked, "What is the faith of democracy . . . except faith in the intelligence of the common man to respond to commonsense to the free play of facts and ideas which are secured by effective guarantees of free inquiry, free assembly, and free communication" (LW 14: 227)? Dewey injected the idea that one of the conditions or social circumstances that fosters personal democracy is peace. Violence, both physical and psychological, is antithetical to democracy. So, peace is a moral condition for the expression of a truly democratic faith and the grounds for genuine discussions that lead to understanding and mutual growth. Thus, he concluded that democratic faith involves a confidence in "the possibility of conducting disputes, controversies and conflicts as cooperative undertakings in which both [or several] parties learn by giving the other a chance to express itself, instead of having one party conquer by forceful suppression of the other—a suppression which is none the less one of violence when it takes place by psychological means of ridicule, abuse, intimidation, instead of overt imprisonment or in concentration camps" (LW 14: 228).

In short, then, Dewey argued that an experiential and procedural process is a part of an authentic democratic faith. The process—of considering the interests and interpretations of others, listening to their concerns and needs, including different parties in discussions and disputes, examining purported facts and opinions presented by everyone, acting to promote equity and fairness for all classes and groups,

and setting into place safeguards and structures for representative communication and involvement in the future—is essential to a democratic personal way of life that informs and energizes a social way of life which, in turn, helps conceptualize and fortify a democratic political way of life. Education, therefore, plays an important role in developing the process and the practice of democracy as it fosters reflective thinkers about the complexities of a democracy. Candidly, he concluded that the processes of living, being educated, and experiencing democracy are invaluable: "[T]he process of experience is more important than any special result attained, so that special results achieved are of ultimate value only as they are used to enrich and order the ongoing process. Since the process of experience is capable of being educative, faith in democracy is all one with faith in experience and education" (LW 14: 229).

A Conception of Education

Not surprisingly, Dewey believed we are obligated to keep recreating democracy by "deliberate and determined endeavor" or "conscious and resolute effort" (LW 14: 225, 224). Deliberate and determined efforts need to be in all political and social settings if personal attitudes are to be sustained and cultivated. However, in his mind, some of the key places for conscious and determined democratic endeavors include our schools and other educational agencies. The connection between education and democracy is a vital one, so vital that they are ultimately inseparable. Democracy, he believed, has a short lifespan and "has to be born anew every generation," something that will not happen without its midwife, education (MW 10: 139). Education, he continued, impregnates society with many ethical principles and concepts, including a common purpose, a purpose that takes into consideration others and their interests. As a result, it is critical that we understand that in a diverse and complex society, the "ability to understand and sympathize with the operations and lot of others is a condition of common purpose which only education can procure," he concluded. He cautioned that "the external differences of pursuit and experience are so very great in our complicated industrial civilization, that men [and women] will not see across and through the walls which separate them, unless they have been trained to do so" (MW 10: 139). We might wish to ask why Dewey believed education is—or at least can be—so powerful, so transformative? Why did he have such a strong faith in education as well as people and democracy? Understanding his conception of education helps us better understand his threefold faith.

Dewey recognized, of course, that democracy, people, and education have weaknesses as well as strengths and offer limitations as well as opportunities. Democracy is neither perfect nor a panacea. Conversely, he believed that a genuine education in a maturing and expanding democracy offers individuals and societies more opportunities for personal and social growth than any other kind of social and governmental arrangement. More precisely, he asserted that the freedoms of the mind, expression, teaching, learning, and intelligence are linked and demand a democratic society and school for their cultivation, manifestation, realization, and continuation (LW 11: 376–380). Hence, we need to examine, criticize, protect, and recreate our freedoms rather than merely assume that they will naturally sustain, perpetuate, and update themselves. To lose or block these freedoms would be a crime against democracy and education and would ignore the "kind of intelligent citizenship that is genuinely free to take part in the social reconstructions without which democracy will die" (LW 11: 378).

However, he feared, in addition to the traditional attempts to restrict and restrain reflective thinking on the part of teachers and students, an endeavor that is largely invisible and highly influential: "It is the attempt to close the minds, mouths, and ears of students and teachers alike to all that is not consonant with the practices and beliefs of the

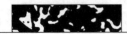

privileged class that represents the economic and political status quo" (LW 11: 377). We may be taken back by his comment and ask: How do economically and politically privileged or powerful people attempt to close the minds of students and teachers? According to Dewey, economically and politically controlling persons use any number of techniques to close minds, including exercising influence over the values and emphases of the curriculum—its ecological, anthropological, pedagogical, and epistemological dimensions—and manipulating school board members, policy-makers, publishers, and parents. The minds of many teachers—and so their students—can also be controlled in part by governmental agencies prescribing employment and accountability conditions for schools. The hurried and regulated life of teachers may leave them little time to think and to nurture their students' thinking. Prescribing the curriculum, teaching, and goals of teachers, then, is one of many means of controlling them—by narrowing the range of their thinking and behavior. Even so, it is not just the privileged who seek to control our minds. Others who lack but want power and who seek privilege may unwittingly be in the mind control business, too.

Education, for Dewey, is a means of fostering reflective thinking, living, working, and teaching. It is a way of promoting ongoing personal, social, and professional growth, a way to live and work productively in a democracy. So, "education is all one with growing; it has no end beyond itself. The criterion of the value of school education is the extent in which it creates a desire for continued growth and supplies means for making the desire effective in fact" (MW 9: 58). Predictably, therefore, "the inclination to learn from life itself and to make the conditions of life such that all will learn in the process of living is the finest product of schooling" (MW 9: 56). Schools, as a result, should provide learning experiences that involve processes of growth that keep fostering greater capacity for enduring growth in the future (MW 9: 59). From these emphases, we see that familial, community, and societal as well as district, school, and classroom environments need to work together to promote the growth of each child. The school alone is insufficiently powerful when other environments are essentially anti-educative and miseducative (MW 9: 7, 15–16). However, if society and school work together, they can provide environments for present and future growth (MW 9: 60–61). Growth, nevertheless, is not related exclusively to work or professional matters. Instead, it, and so education, ought to address the whole person, attempting to promote each individual's development into a "unified personality" (LW 8: 71) and to use and further the capacities and interests of everyone:

> The best guarantee of collective efficiency and power is liberation and use of the diversity of individual capacities in initiative, planning, foresight, vigor and endurance. Personality must be educated, and personality cannot be educated by confining its operations to technical and specialized things, or to the less important relationships of life. Full education comes only when there is a responsible share on the part of each person, in proportion to capacity, in shaping the aims and policies of the social groups to which he belongs. This fact fixes the significance of democracy. (MW 12:199)

Democracy, then, is not an external ingredient to education. Instead, "Democracy is itself an educational principle, an educational measure and policy" (LW 13: 294). That is to say, the practice of democracy in schools—a form of schooling that is governed by freedom of thought and exploration, respect for persons and evidence, concern for others and arguments, appreciation of diversity and commonalities, and so forth—is intrinsic to the nature of education. Education without democracy is thin, at best, and it may shrivel into indoctrination and authoritarianism over time.

Growth is also at the heart of Dewey's thoughts about "a constant reorganizing or reconstructing" of our experience, e.g., our thinking, feeling, and liv-

ing (MW 9: 82). This reconstruction of experience ought to be enriching, not stratifying and narrowing. This belief led him to a technical definition of education: "It is that reconstruction or reorganization of experience which adds to the meaning of experience, and which increases ability to direct the course of subsequent experience" (MW 9: 82). Would we be better off without a technical definition? It can prove helpful. For instance, we can readily add and appreciate ideas from his other writings:

- We have experiences, and we create or construct meanings or interpretations out of and with them.
- Education provides additional experience which enables us to learn more and revisit our earlier experience.
- Revisiting our prior experience with new understanding allows us to *re*organize our thinking or *re*construct our meanings or interpretations.
- Experience after experience, if reflected upon, adds to our understanding of life and enables us to interpret or make sense of other experiences.
- Education should take us beyond our usual paths to expand our understanding of the experiences of others and the world of formal inquiry.
- Learning from new and diverse experiences enhances the meaning and pleasure we can derive from life.
- Continuous learning via educative experiences provides us with new and refined abilities and understandings that can direct or control our later experiences.
- Educative experiences demand a freedom and a set of environments built on personal respect and individual guidance for learning.

In view of these matters, he argued for an educational standard that centers on the student's capacity to keep growing: "The best thing that can be said about any special process of education, like that of the formal school period, is that it renders its subject capable of further education: more sensitive to

conditions of growth and more able to take advantage of them" (MW 12: 185).

The responsibilities of educators in democratically oriented schools are complex and require attention to using a special kind of learning experiences and learning environments as a part of the formal curriculum. Just having students and things in a classroom does not count. What students experience does matter. In particular, Dewey suggested, "The educator's part in the enterprise of education is to furnish the environment which stimulates responses and directs the learner's course. In last analysis, all that the educator can do is modify stimuli so that response will as surely as is possible result in the formation of desirable intellectual and emotional dispositions" (MW 9:188). In addition, this requires teachers, in Dewey's mind, to assist students as they learn to think reflectively. Moreover, students need to learn to think about how we think and how and why we act the way we do, not just cultivate good habits, skills, and practices. Naturally, theories of knowledge and of ethics should be the result of democratic inquiries and debates or research and reason, not privately assumed stances that lack public data, analysis, rationales, and dialogue. They are implicitly in any curriculum and should be intrinsic aspects of the formal curriculum. Issues regarding claims of knowledge—whether about history, science, art, mathematics, ethics—are vital parts of the school curriculum, not separate problems that are imported into discussions.

A Theory of Knowledge

Dewey's theory of knowledge, comparable to many of his other ideas, has been variously described. In chapter 2, we noted that his viewpoint is a modified *perspectivist* one. In part, this description is merited because he thought that no one ever approaches a question of knowledge or truth with "a virgin mind" (LW 8: 214). Also, he believed that gender, cultural, religious, and even scientific perspectives influence and sometimes determine what a person understands as facts and how they are interpreted.

However, he also thought that reflective thinking and democratic dialogue can help us identify commonalities as well as gain an understanding of different viewpoints. By reflecting openly together, we can examine the relevant facts and reasons for views and often be brought closer together in our interpretations and beliefs. Even so, he knew complete unanimity of thought was undesirable and cautioned against forcing or imposing a single point of view on one another. Indeed, he not only encouraged tolerance of diverse ideas but actually stressed that even in the development of a science of education there was a need for multiple sciences, not adherence to a single science of education (LW 3: 259–261). In chapter 3, we also observed that Dewey compared thinking from different perspectives to climbing mountains to gain vantage spots. His conclusion was that no one can simultaneously climb a number of mountains but can scale them separately to gain a broader understanding. His analogy and other writings indicate that the different mountain viewpoints "supplement one another: they do not set up incompatible, competing worlds" (MW 9: 117). He was aware, of course, that people will not always see the same things from even the same mountains, but his interest in this context was on gaining multiple perspectives on the same concerns or issues. The individual needs to develop multiple perspectives in order to see more clearly. Competing views of the world did not trouble him, for he believed that the disagreement can and, ideally, does lead to a greater depth and breadth of understanding that enables people to appreciate diverse paradigms.

His theory of knowledge is also sometimes described as **falliblist** and **constructivist.** The first term is a reference to his idea that what we can genuinely claim to know needs to be tempered by our capacity to know and the nature of the universe. The second word, *constructivist,* is an allusion to the process of constructing knowledge. That is to say, a person constructs her knowledge out of the ideas, experiences, views, data, and reasons she examines and

Falliblist

a word that suggests that we sometimes make mistakes when we claim to know something and that we should be more guarded about our assertions about knowing

Constructivist

a term that suggests that a person constructs knowledge out of the ideas, experiences, views, data, and reasons that are available to her

the hypotheses she tests. In other words, he believed that we are incapable of knowing with absolute certainty, because our capacity to know is limited, our claims to knowledge are frequently based on conclusions that others have reached and of which we cannot rightly claim to know, the construction of knowledge is an ongoing project and involves revising or rebuilding our knowledge claims as we learn more, and the universe and society continue to change as dynamic entities and qualify what we can claim to know. Consequently, we should be cautious when we talk about knowledge and truth. If we speak precisely, we may use **warranted assertibility** instead of *knowledge* to clarify that our claims are warranted, if they are, at the time we speak with the facts, data, and reasons we have and understand (LW 14: 168). We are warranted in making assertions or truth claims when the bases for such claims are a growing body of relevant and tested hypotheses and reflections that corroborate them. Our *conviction* about acting on what we understand should be in proportion to the strength of the warrant for our claims (LW 8: 74, 98). Our truth claims, in turn, are "hypotheses" that need to be tested (LW 8:74) and held in such a way that we continue to learn from additional experiences and inquiry (LW 8: 98).

The pursuit of warranted claims, while a personal matter, is also a public one. The evolving body of supportive data and analysis, though done by individuals, is not a work of individualistic inquiry. In a society where there is open inquiry and debate, further deliberation and confirmation are required. The growth of knowledge—or, rather, of warranted assertions—is an open and public adventure that takes considerable time and involves a number of people. In *The Public and Its Problems* (1927), Dewey more fully clarified what he meant by knowledge or warranted assertions being a public affair. He wrote that knowledge "is a function of association and communication; it depends upon tradition, upon tools and methods socially transmitted, developed and sanctioned. Faculties of effectual observation,

Warranted assertibility
a phrase that Dewey preferred to the word "knowledge" to emphasize the fact that reflective people should look for rational and evidentiary grounds or warrants of beliefs

reflection and desire are habits acquired under the influence of the culture and institutions of society, not ready-made inherent powers" (LW 2: 334).

Focusing on this last quotation for a few moments, we learn, first, that we cannot be assured that truth claims are warranted until they have been shared with, tested, and confirmed by others. They take place in a community of inquirers, scholars, and researchers who share a tradition of inquiry. As Dewey said, they are "a function of association and communication" (LW 2: 334). The claims we want to call warranted or true still remain hypotheses or instruments for attaining additional truth (MW 6: 12ff), even when they are appropriately examined, replicated, and confirmed by others. The word **instrumentalist** is, therefore, also associated with Dewey's theory of knowledge: assertions—when tested and verified—are ideally instruments for further inquiry and of arriving at additional warranted conclusions. Second, we learn that our methods of testing and confirming hypotheses are socially developed, conveyed, and approved. Over time, often centuries, people have developed reflective approaches for inquiry and examination of claims, and "truth *denotes* verified beliefs, propositions that have emerged from a certain procedure of inquiry and testing" (MW 6: 28). Importantly, then, both the methods and the conclusions of inquiry are confirmed in the public activity of pursuing truth claims. The public nature of methods and conclusions, though, leaves them open to further examination, refinement, and, when warranted, rejection. Third, the habits of observation and reflection are socially transmitted, not individually determined, and are human constructions that may be revised for sound reasons just as may our methods of inquiry and our conclusions. Inquiry and arriving at warranted assertions are dynamic social undertakings.

Given this Deweyan frame of reference, then, our claims to know should be based on an understanding that these claims are, at best, perspectival, provisional, partial, and, at times, probable. However,

---

Instrumentalist

a person, such as Dewey, who thinks that the best warranted truth claims are those that can be used as instruments for further inquiry and enable us to arrive at additional warranted conclusions the best warranted assertions have been examined and, so far, have stood up to examination better than other claims. They are characterized by degrees of warrant or security, not certainty (LW 14: 171). In addition, we need a certain openness of mind about them, but we should not act as if we knew nothing. Better yet, we should not think and act as if the warrant for *all* truth claims is always weak or inadequate or purely perspectival. We have gradations of warrant for claims. The propositions with strongest degrees of warrant—"propositions have been so frequently verified without failure that we are justified in using them as if they were absolutely true"—ought to be acted upon (LW 2: 12). However, Dewey argued, as we reflect and learn and act, we should not forget that "logically absolute truth is an ideal which cannot be realized" (LW 2: 12). We ought, therefore, to abandon the quest for logical absolute certainty and pursue understanding that is based upon experimentally warranted and secure conclusions (LW 4).

Dewey moved easily from his theories of knowledge and reflection to his theories of instruction and educative experience as he summarized his views of thinking in *Democracy and Education*. His extended comment is worth repeating.

> Processes of instruction are unified in the degree in which they centre in the production of good habits of thinking. While we may speak, without error, of the method of thought, the important thing is that thinking is the method of an educative experience. The essentials of method are therefore identical with the essentials of reflection. They are [1] first that the pupil have a genuine situation of experience—that there be a continuous activity in which he is interested for its own sake; [2] secondly, that a genuine problem develop within this situation as a stimulus to thought; [3] third, that he possess the information and make the observations needed to deal with it; [4] fourth, that suggested solutions occur to him which he shall be responsible for developing in an orderly way; [5] fifth, that he have opportunity and occasion to test his ideas by application, to make their

meaning clear and to discover for himself their validity. (MW 9: 170)

We learn to think well by thinking well, by practicing good thinking with others as we have indicated in chapter 2. Thoughtfully planned group learning activities, therefore, had multiple values for Dewey. When so conceptualized and practiced, they are consistent with, or, in fact, identical to both the scientific or reflective method of inquiry and democratic living. Learning is a social experience whose theories and practices, as in any other area of life, may be challenged or confirmed by members of the learning community. The five phases of reflection and instruction, however, are not necessarily procedurally sequential or prescribed. Indeed, a class or student may begin at one of the so-called higher numbered phases and realize that they need to move to other phases in a flexible manner. Fundamentally, this approach to reflection needs to be critically used if we are to develop thoughtful people in all areas of life. In addition, these phases need to be interpreted in the context of what Dewey stated elsewhere about the reflective person (see chapter 2).

A Theory of Ethics

Some who have only picked up pieces of Dewey's ethical thought consider his views either a form of ethical subjectivism (that ethical beliefs and choices are purely a matter of personal preferences) or a type of ethical relativism (that ethical beliefs and choices are relative to or determined exclusively by the context or culture in which one lives). Many of Dewey's comments—when decontextualized—can lead to either interpretation. Certainly, he emphasized the uniqueness of making an ethical decision (MW 12: 176), the necessity of considering contextual information (MW 12: 176), and the inevitability of personally weighing the importance of ethical principles (LW 7: 232ff). These comments, however, are just a few of the pieces of the complex ethical theory that Dewey offered, a theory that requires knowledge, reflection, and imagination, not simply the blind pursuit of our personal wishes or an unthinking adherence to our cultural or group mores. His ethical theory, therefore, like his theory of knowledge, involves a democratic commitment where claims are debated and tested until they become warranted (LW 8: 76).

Instead of promoting either a naïve subjectivism or a crude relativism, Dewey emphasized reflection in his thoughts about ethics: We ought to be reflective thinkers about ethical issues, decisions, and living, not act instinctively or automatically on our personal or cultural tastes. Ethical thinking needs to take into consideration, first, that ethical choices are unique because no two individuals and situations are precisely alike. They are unique like snowflakes. However, claiming that ethical decisions are unique is not the same as saying they are entirely an individual matter. Both snowflakes and ethical choices are open to scientific investigation. Second, the situation in which a decision is made is part of what makes the choice unique: *The details* of the ethical choice matter. For him, to ignore the facts of an ethical issue is intellectually irresponsible, not reflective. Even so, to claim that considering a particular situation is vital to reaching an ethical decision is different from claiming that the situation prescribes or determines one's decision, although it may limit one's options. Facts may in part define or determine the problem or issues, but ethics is about what to do about the situation or facts. And the facts do not speak for themselves but have to be interpreted in the light of a larger theory. Third, Dewey focused on the uniqueness of the situation and the decision in order to argue that we need to consider, project, and discover—yes, *discover*—what a good outcome is likely to be. We consider as we reflect upon a wide variety of information, evidence, and ideas. By studying, we *discover* the details involved. By *projecting* possible outcomes of alternative courses of action—what is good—we also learn more about what our choice should be. While we are seeking to

determine what the good is, we keep in mind the "specific ill" or "exact defect" we wish to avoid (MW 12: 176). Clearly, then, Dewey was not saying we should think in one or more of the following ways: First, do whatever you prefer because ethical choices are merely personal preferences; second, do whatever the culture indicates is appropriate because all values are merely cultural constructs, or, third, do whatever the context indicates is good (LW 7: 230). Conversely, Dewey was saying that, first, ethical issues help us identify more precisely ills and evils we want to avoid; second, ethical situations are unique and need to be carefully studied; third, potential outcomes of choices need to be imagined and analyzed, and, fourth, ethical decisions are important and should not be taken lightly.

Even so, many think his position is weak when it comes to informing us about how we decide which outcomes are worthwhile and how we can justify the outcomes we select (Menand, 375). This criticism is partially deserved, although Dewey did tell us more than some critics suggest. For example, he informed us that growth is the end of morality as it is for education as a moral endeavor and that the process of growing is "the significant thing," not "health as an end fixed once and for all, but the needed improvement in health—a continual process—is the end and good. The end is no longer a terminus or limit to be reached. It is the active process of transforming the existent situation. Not perfection as a final goal, but the ever-enduring process of perfecting, maturing, refining is the aim in living" (MW 12: 181).

He also acknowledged that "honesty, industry, temperance, justice" provide us with indicators of the ongoing process or "directions of change in the quality of experience," but that they are not "fixed ends" that can be achieved (MW 12: 181). Thus, the bad person is the one who is "beginning to deteriorate, to grow less good" and the good person is the one who "is moving to become better" (MW 12:180–181). Of course, he claimed very early in life that democracy is "an ethical conception, and upon its ethical significance" we find its governmental, social, and personal importance (EW 1: 240). Later in life he restated the cardinal role democracy "provides [as] a moral standard for personal conduct" (LW 13: 155). Of course, he associated a variety of values with democratic communities, including freedom of thought—"the root of all freedom" (LW 11: 378)—and the freedoms of religion, speech, press, assembly, and petition (LW 11: 252). Justice, impartiality, equity, and toleration are likewise values that direct us in the process of growth (LW 7: 279, 231) but that cannot become final, absolute ends because we are forever learning about these values and how they need to be interpreted in a changing society and universe. He also believed that financial and cultural freedoms are needed for "the release of the human spirit in all its capacities for development through science, art, and unconstrained human intercourse" (LW 11: 253). So, Dewey observed that, up to the time he was writing, a democratic community is "the best means" we have available for political, social, and personal development (LW 11: 217–218)—though nothing he said suggests he thought democracy will be superseded. He further thought that those who have experienced or studied democratic and undemocratic governments and societies usually prefer "democratic and humane arrangements to those which are autocratic and harsh" (LW 13: 17) and asked three questions:

> [1] Can we find any reason that does not ultimately come down to the belief that democratic social arrangements promote a better quality of human experience, one which is more widely accessible and enjoyed, than do non-democratic and anti-democratic forms of social life? [2] Does not the principle of regard for individual freedom and for decency and kindliness of human relations come back in the end to the conviction that these things are tributary to a higher quality of experience on the part of a greater number than are methods of repression and coercion or force? [3] Is it not the reason for our preference that we believe that mutual consultation and convictions reached

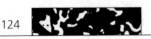

through persuasion, make possible a better quality of experience than can otherwise be provided
on any wide scale? (LW 13: 18)

Does this mean that those who live in a democracy should ignore everything except agreed-upon
democratic values? For Dewey, the answer was clearly
no. His answer stemmed from what he saw as a
growing body of knowledge that is often relevant to
ethical decisions, even though they are invariably
unique and situational. We can learn a great deal as
we think about prior experiences and issues that
will be useful: We can, first, compare different ethical cases and gain important insights from them, second, develop a collection of morally harmful behaviors
and determine why they arise and how they are
destructive, and, third, generalize about the related
goods we identify and wish to nurture (MW 12:
176). However, we must remember that "the value
of this systematization is intellectual or analytic"; it
does not dictate or prescribe in detail what we should
do (MW 12: 176). Instead, systematized knowledge
helps us analyze issues better—think more clearly, intelligently, evidentially, imaginatively, contextually,
rationally—by suggesting important human traits,
possibilities, and methods of solving problems.
Knowledge—warranted assertions—suggests hypotheses to examine and outcomes to scrutinize. Data
"are tools of insight" and promote intelligent decision making by individuals and groups (MW 12:
176–177). In effect, therefore, prior learning helps us
develop fruitful approaches to ethical questions,
including "methods of inquiry to locate difficulties
and evils; methods . . . to form plans to be used as
working hypotheses in dealing with them" (MW
12:177). If we do not use prior learning, we are in reality discarding our minds.

The scientific research that is needed to construct broad bodies of knowledge that inform ethical thinking is what we would expect from Dewey's
overall theory of knowledge: "Inquiry, discovery
take the same place in morals that they have come
to occupy in sciences of nature. Validation, demon-

stration become experimental, a matter of consequences" (MW 12: 179). His experimental approach to ethics places emphasis on doing research—in the broad sense of gathering information and data—to discover the variety and consequences of different customs, traditions, laws, policies, procedures, and practices. Reason—informed by relevant studies, experiences, and imagination—picks up the task of examining "the needs and conditions, the obstacles and resources, of situations" and helps develop plans that assist in overcoming the problems identified, e.g., inequity and injustice, restriction and suppression, oppression and exploitation, hunger and sickness, and homelessness and unemployment (MW 12: 179). This research and reflection, therefore, provide part of the data and insight that are needed to think critically and carefully about specific ethical issues. To engage in reflective ethical reasoning, however, we need to attend to *situations* that involve an ethical challenge. This further, specific inquiry is necessary precisely because each situation is unique and needs to be examined both for its commonalities with prior cases and its differences as an individual case. Thus, case-specific research—or research related to a particular current ethical case—is needed, even though background research has already been completed, and there are a number of ethical principles that appear relevant. In attempting to resolve a particular problem, therefore, it is imperative that we keep in mind that fresh, situation-specific thinking is needed although there are "principles, criteria, laws [that] are intellectual instruments" which remain useful for analyzing these "unique situations" (MW 12: 173). Among other considerations, we need to contemplate the future—possible and probable—consequences of our actions on others and ourselves. So, past decisions and existing principles can never "be wholly relied upon to justify a course of action. No amount of pains taken in forming a purpose in a definite case is final; the consequences of its adoption must be carefully noted, and a purpose held only as a working hypothesis

until results confirm its rightness" (MW 12: 179–180).

Pause for a moment to consider the implications of Dewey's ideas for an actual situation. Let us say, for example, that there are consistent and well-developed data that indicate there is a pattern of employment discrimination against overweight women. Employers are inclined, intentionally or otherwise, to offer positions to men rather than women and to women who weigh less than other women of similar height and body type—except for, say, the anorexic—even when they are less well qualified than heavier people. Suppose too that it has been determined that size or weight has little or no influence on job performance as, say, a teacher. When accused of discriminatory hiring practices by an applicant, a school district human resource person might respond by saying that unfairness just did not happen, that she is aware of related research, and the district had previously decided to ensure that it would continue to follow fair employment practices by developing and implementing a new plan. The newly implemented plan is designed to continue fair hiring practices. Moreover, she says that the applicant in question was not discriminated against because all applicants' skills, abilities, and performance indicators are evaluated by a committee who saw and evaluated them and the actual hiring was done by a person who did not see the applicants. The person doing the hiring made a judgment based on, among other considerations, recorded scores and interview answers. In addition, written references and prior performance evaluations were used by the person. Finally, the written observations of the interviewing committee were also taken into consideration, but nothing was said or written about the weight of the candidate filing a complaint. Dewey might say that these claims are relevant to determining if a fair employment decision was made in this particular case but that more inquiry may be needed.

If we act as Dewey would like us to, we may examine the broader research literature on teacher hiring practices, the data on the particular district doing the hiring, and the history of the person who actually hires teachers for the school in question. The school board's research and established ethical principles of fairness are relevant, but what have been the consequences of the district's plan? Good intentions or, as Dewey said, purposes, are insufficient. Consequences must be considered. The district hypothesized that its plan would avoid discriminatory hiring practices. However, is the hypothesis substantiated when tested? Examining data since the plan was implemented, interviewing existing district personnel, studying the data on applicants who were and were not offered positions, and other steps will help determine whether the district did or did not discriminate in the specific case. Still, the particular situation is unique. We need to know, if possible, what happened in *this specific case and context.* Did anything unethical occur with regard to *this applicant?* Dewey claimed, "We are only pleading for the adoption in moral reflection of the logic that has been proved to make security, stringency and fertility in passing judgments upon physical phenomena" (MW 12: 174).

Dewey was aware that the outcomes of ethical choices are not always desirable, much less desired. Reasons for the undesirable results are manifold, including at a minimum the lack of background research on the issue, the inadequate ethical understanding of individuals involved, the paucity of any case-specific data or information, and the character of the person making decisions. We can be misled and ill-informed, and we can conceal our motives and destroy relevant data.

Where, then, does Dewey's ethical thinking lead us? Just as democracy is political, social, and personal, so is being ethical, a critical feature of a democratic society. Legal structures and societal interactions help build environments that promote ethical choices and living. Education enables a person to reflect on moral problems and consider ethical decisions. Even so, more is needed if the values of a democratic com-

munity are to be manifested in personal behavior: the commitment of individual persons to being ethical is crucial. Thus, the personal character of people—their "virtues and moral excellencies"—is a primary concern for him (MW 12:174). Personal character, like personal democracy, ought not to be ignored by schools or society. "Our moral failures," he believed, "go back to some weakness of disposition, some absence of sympathy, some one-sided bias that makes us perform the judgment of the concrete case carelessly" or defiantly (MW 12: 173). If we are going to address these failures, educational agencies—schools, homes, businesses, and so forth—need to develop people who have, among other qualities, "wide sympathy, keen sensitiveness, persistence in the face of the disagreeable, balance of interests enabling [them] . . . to undertake the work of analysis and decision intelligently" (MW 12: 173–174). In the end, therefore, "the only guarantee of impartial, disinterested inquiry is the social sensitiveness of the inquirer to the needs and problems of those with whom he is associated" (MW 12: 165). Dewey's ideal of "disinterested and impartial inquiry," of course, is a process, not a destination (MW 12: 164): those who pursue understanding of a specific issue should have "no particular end set up in advance so as to shut in the activities of observation, forming of ideas, and application" (MW 12: 164). The goal of impartial inquiry, in spite of human and cultural tendencies to the contrary, amounts to an attempt to liberate ourselves from our biases via public examination of controversies and requires that we "attend to every fact that is relevant to defining the problem or need, and to follow up every suggestion that promises a clue" (MW 12: 164). Public inquiry, at times, comes in the form of appeals of school personnel decisions.

Dewey added that, even if universal values were metaphysically or logically possible, they could not take us very far. The existential realities of living are more persuasive, and the only way of "universalizing the moral law"—such as freedom, justice, sympathy, equal respect—is through extensive democratic interaction, communication, and participation (MW 12: 197). "The counterpart of this proposition is that the situation in which a good is consciously realized is not one of transient sensations or private appetites but one of sharing and communication—public, social" (MW 12: 197–198). "Universalization means socialization, the extension of the area and range of those who share in a good" (MW 12: 198). Ethical thinking, then, is an open endeavor based on publicly pursued and debated values, principles, research, inquiry, and reflection. Any time that members of the public determine that location, bias, incompetence, or lack of commitment to finding information and thinking have influenced the decisions of others, they have the responsibility to challenge the conclusions and to work toward a more warranted end.

Consistent with his theory of knowledge, Dewey maintained that both initial conclusions and counterarguments may be flawed in part or in their entirety and for many reasons. In cases like this, the solution is to return to the information, data, and claims to explore, experiment, and reflect. This approach is necessary as no person or group—including the entire human race—can claim to have arrived at the absolute truth on any ethical issue because only provisional truth can be determined (LW 2: 12). Provisional truth, though, should not be treated lightly, trivialized, or dismissed for, as in other fields, it may be secure even if it is not absolutely certain. It is the best substantiated and warranted knowledge that we have. To ignore it would be similar to dismissing our knowledge of the consequences of contracting AIDS or eating contaminated foods. Indeed, knowledge or warranted conclusions may be so secure—because of repeated experiments and verifications—that we can use it as if it were "absolutely true" (LW 2: 12).

This claim of being able to find and use secure knowledge "as if" it were absolutely true may cause us to pause but may also help explain why Dewey

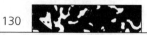

distinguished between two types of moral struggle. The first kind of struggle occurs "when an individual is tempted to do something which he [or she] is convinced is wrong" (LW 7: 164), such as whether to award a student a higher grade to avoid seeing her parents again, hire the superintendent's son instead of a better qualified applicant, or buy an extra book with school funds so it can be given to one's daughter at home. Plausible "*as if* absolutely true" ethical statements for educators may include a number of prescriptions or prohibitions: such as, it is wrong to physically abuse students, all students should be treated with equal respect, and each person should be encouraged to think for herself. While for all practical purposes we know full well what is wrong or right in these cases, even these are not completely beyond question and must be reflected on and intelligently studied, not mindlessly dictated. The second kind of ethical struggle, where ethical warrant or knowledge is not so clear, is about how to make judgments between competing goods, values, and duties (LW 7: 164–165), e.g., whether it would be better to designate monies for health promotion or educational travel, build a new middle school or renovate a high school, or devote more resources to the science program or to the music program.

Three additional aspects of Dewey's ethical theory merit attention: first, the sources of knowledge for ethical reflection, second, the role of ethical principles in ethical reasoning, and, third, the function of dramatic or imaginative rehearsal in ethical decision making. Concerning the first, the sources of knowledge for ethical reflection, Dewey did not think ethics was a moral science which was "a separate province" but instead one informed by many forms of inquiry, including but not limited to biology, chemistry, history, medicine, anthropology, psychology, engineering, physiology, and statistics (MW 14: 204). He also observed that ethical thinking may profit from studying judicial, legislative, legal, and historical events and decisions. Similarly and perhaps today surprisingly, "codes of conduct" may serve as "a storehouse of information and possible indications of what is now right and good" (LW 7: 179). Knowledge from these fields—indeed, anything "that can be known of the human mind and body," literature and arts as much as science— "enables us to understand the conditions and agencies through which man lives, and on account of which he forms and executes his plans" (MW 14: 204). It illuminates and provides guidance for thinking, deciding, and acting (MW 14: 205). These "empirical facts" about nature, society, and human beings are crucial to understand because we live and interact in an environment, and "it is not 'in' that environment as coins are in a box, but as a plant is in the sunlight and soil. It is of them, continuous with their energies, dependent upon their support, capable of increase only as it utilizes them, and as it gradually rebuilds from their crude indifference an environment genially civilized"(MW 14: 204).

This approach to examining information and data should not make us subservient to tradition. Only intelligence—thinking that is informed by relevant information and a consideration of the consequences of acting on the knowledge—can tell us "when to use the fact to conform and perpetuate [environments], and when to use it to vary conditions and consequences" (MW 14: 206). In thinking about the implications of facts and other ethical considerations, Dewey warned against ideological blinders, especially those of a privileged class that takes "every means, even to a monopoly of moral ideals, to carry on its struggle for class-power" (MW 14: 208). Public inquiry into ethical issues should bring an end to power- and class-based decision making. Because education is permeated with ethical choices regarding desirable behaviors, dispositions, and consequences that are contested by different social and ideological groups, educators cannot be mere spectators. They cannot be neutral about the moral development of students and society in a democracy (MW 14: 193–195).

Second, we consider Dewey's interpretation of ethical principles and the role they play in ethical think-

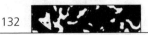

ing (LW 7: 275ff). Ethical thinking, rooted in forms of inquiry, experiential understanding, moral values, democratic ideals, and reflective investigations, leads to a careful consideration of the diverse situations in which we find ourselves. As we deliberate and make judgments, we learn that there are common elements and similar values in various situations. Discrimination, for instance, may have some common elements whether it is against Latinos, African Americans, Native Americans, Arab Americans, European Americans, or Asian Americans. Seeing these common elements helps us recognize that "general ideas are a great aid in judging particular cases," for "experience is intellectually cumulative" and may eventually extend to and include different ideas and values from various peoples and cultures of the world (LW 7: 275). As he noted,

> Out of resembling experiences general ideas develop; through language, instruction, and tradition this gathering together of experiences of value into generalized points of view is extended to take in a whole people and a race [or the world population]. Through intercommunication the experience of the entire human race is to some extent pooled and crystallized in general ideas. These ideas constitute principles. We bring them with us to deliberation on particular situations. These generalized points of view are of great use in surveying particular cases. (LW 7: 275–276)

Principles, however, may become decontextualized and, thereby, turned into rules. Then, they are wrongly treated as ends in themselves, not as "aids and instruments in judging values" (LW 7: 276). The differences between an ethical rule (which Dewey rejected) and an ethical principle (which he embraced) are crucial and, so, two major differences should not be forgotten. First, "a principle evolves in connection with the course of experience, being a generalized statement of what sort of consequences and values tend to be realized in certain kinds of situations; a rule is taken as something ready-made and fixed" (LW 7: 276). Second, "a principle is primarily intellectual, a method and scheme for judging, and is practical secondarily because of what it discloses; a rule is primarily practical" (LW 7: 276). Ethical principles—as well as pertinent facts and arguments—play an important role in being a reflective thinker: "Unless the pertinence and force of each seemingly evidential fact and seemingly explanatory idea is judged, appraised, the mind goes on a wild-goose chase" (LW 8: 215).

For Dewey, therefore, moral principles were intellectual tools or methods that help us think through moral problems using, but not uncritically, the wisdom that has been gained from the experience of many peoples, not a private or group tool for personal, class, racial, gender, or cultural advantage. A moral principle provides a person with a basis for studying and analyzing specific issues and cases. In essence,

> [1] It holds before him certain possible aspects of the act; [2] it warns him against taking a short or partial view of the act. [3] It economizes his thinking by supplying him with the main heads by reference to which to consider the bearings of his desires and purposes; [4] it guides him in his thinking by suggesting to him the important considerations for which he should be on the lookout. (LW 7: 280)

Considering the interests of others, tolerating cultural differences, granting freedom of speech, respecting diverse peoples, telling the truth, allowing for different religious beliefs, defending the rights of others, and so forth are principles for Dewey. They provide an inherited and warranted framework of ideas with which to analyze and think about issues in the present. Some may be insightful and helpful at times; others will not. However, they are not rules for closing contemporary discussions and debates. They do not silence people but initiate reflections, discussions, and judgments.

Third, the role of dramatic or imaginative rehearsal in ethical theory was of great importance to Dewey. Rehearsal, for him, is more than an intellectual exercise: It distinctly helps the person involved *feel* the potential consequences and, therefore, develop responsibility for her thoughts, decisions, and actions.

The rehearsal dramatizes the fact that the person doing the choosing and acting is involved in creating her own dispositions and habits, too. As a matter of fact, she is "making a difference in the [or her] *self,* as determining what one will *be*" (LW 7: 274). She learns that the "choice at stake in moral deliberation or valuation is the worth of this and that kind of character and disposition" (LW 7: 274). When her choices and actions become her habitual way of living and being, she will be a particular kind of person. Reflection or deliberation on ethical options, then, is "dramatic and active" and "has the intuitive, the direct factor in it" (LW 7: 275). The advantages of **dramatic rehearsal** over an actual trial are that, first, it "is retrievable, whereas overt consequences" are not and, second, "many trials may mentally be made in a short time" (LW 7: 275).

Of course, in dramatic rehearsal, an accurate understanding of likely consequences is invaluable. Indirectly, the person involved in a dramatic rehearsal of ethical decision making also comes to better understand accountability and responsibility for her choices and their consequences. Dramatic rehearsal, then, provides the opportunity for a person to become a more responsible person. "The individual is *held* accountable for what he *has* done [during dramatic rehearsal] in order that he may be responsive in what he is *going* to do [in actuality]. Gradually, persons learn by dramatic imitation to hold themselves accountable, and liability becomes a voluntary deliberate acknowledgement that deeds are our own, that their consequences come from us" (MW 14: 217).

Dewey's ethical theory, therefore, permeates his view of the school as a place for developing reflective thinkers and a setting that supports and encourages reflection by all involved, be they students, teachers, administrators, or others. A reflective community is the ideal, but reflective practitioners are the heart of a democratic, ethical, and educative community known as school. Reflection alone, though, is inadequate. Students and educators need to develop virtues and dispositions that predispose

Dramatic rehearsal
the idea of testing hypotheses about the future consequences of decisions imaginatively before actually trying them out

them to understand the feelings and interests of others. We need insight into and sympathy for others. We need to develop a sense of responsibility and accountability for the "deeds" that belong to us and the "consequences [that] come from us" (MW 14:217). In short, we need to recognize that our thinking and choosing affect who we and others are in a democratic community.

Conclusion

As we think through Dewey's ideas about democracy, education, knowledge, and ethics, we see several themes or strands of thought. One idea that runs throughout his thoughts is the theme of growth. Growth is a quality or characteristic that Dewey believed is an inherent part of both a healthy democracy and education. Likewise, he believed that warranted theories of knowledge and **ethics** require growth or an ongoing learning that fosters maturity of thought and action. Evolving fields of inquiry, including ethics, are the grounds and impetus for a dynamic democracy and education. A growing person and community is as much a requirement for an educative society as it is for an educative school. Growing intellectually, emotionally, politically, morally, socially, and personally are interwoven, creating the fabric of human development.

Ethics

a field of study that examines the intellectual and evidentiary grounds for conducting moral life in one way rather than another

The road to human development, in this sense, involves learning, but not just any kind of learning. The learning that political, social, and personal democracies require involves, Dewey said, not just developing in knowledge and reflection, but a "cumulative movement of action" (MW 9: 46). Thinking without acting is only one half of the learning cycle. Genuine learning entails both reflection and action. The reflective learner, therefore, needs to be concerned with the development of her attitudes, dispositions, and habits as well as with behavior or actions. Thinking in the light of these matters will enable us to guard against the cultural and personal influences that work together to make us dogmatic (MW 12: 98). The challenge to learn and grow, of

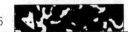
course, is a responsibility of society, too, not just one of schools. If we help build a learning, educative society, we are, in Dewey's mind, all educators. We are co-constructors of a democracy that shares an approach to knowledge, ethical reasoning, and democratic living that helps us rethink and revise governmental structures, informal associations, and personal dispositions along self-governing, independent thinking, and egalitarian lines.

GLOSSARY

Consequences—a word that refers to the outcomes (quantitative and qualitative) of feeling, thinking, and behaving in particular ways that are important in determining their value or worth in school and society.

Constructivist—a term that suggests that a person constructs knowledge out of the ideas, experiences, views, data, and reasons that are available to her.

Dramatic rehearsal—the idea of testing hypotheses about the future consequences of decisions imaginatively before actually trying them out.

Ethics—a field of study that examines the intellectual and evidentiary grounds for conducting moral life in one way rather than another.

Falliblist—a word that suggests that we sometimes make mistakes when we claim to know something and that we should be more guarded about our assertions to know.

Growth—the concept that the development of a person's dispositions and habits of thinking and acting is intrinsically worthwhile and contributes in the present and the future to personal and social development.

Instrumentalist—a person, such as Dewey, who thinks that the best warranted truth claims are those that can be used as instruments for further inquiry and enable us to arrive at additional warranted conclusions.

Knowledge—a common term that often implies that we have convincing reasons and evidence for being absolutely sure that a statement or proposition is true, but for Dewey it meant that we have cogent grounds or are warranted in making a provisional truth claim.

Personal democracy—a reference to a person being so characterized by democratic attitudes, dispositions, habits, and

behaviors that her character is formed by them.

Political democracy—a phrase that alludes to a form or structure of government that is based on the values of freedom, equality, opportunity, tolerance, justice, openness, and participation.

Social democracy—a way of living that is characterized by the enactment of the values of a political democracy and is noted for its common interests, social interactions, and candid communication.

Warranted assertibility—a phrase that Dewey preferred to the word "knowledge" in order to underline the fact that reflective people should look for rational and evidentiary grounds or warrants for beliefs.

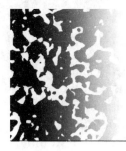

CHAPTER FIVE

Conclusion

As we conclude this primer on John Dewey, there are a myriad of potential closing remarks that could be made and as many questions to be raised, especially if we wish to compare his ideas to contemporary educational thinkers, examine the implications of his thought for present-day issues, or evaluate the strengths and weaknesses of his ideas. Among the many possibilities open to us, we have selected five to pursue. First, it is clear that Dewey was an educational crank in many ways during his time. His rejection of inadequate educational theory and practice was not an accident. His critique of philosophical and political trends informed and complemented his reflective remarks about education and schooling. Moreover, it is not strange, in some ways, to find his thinking at odds with many present-day educational and political pronouncements and practices. Indeed, his questions and ideas, because they are focused on critical and long-standing educational and political questions and issues, remain relevant today. However, the relevance of his ideas is notewor-

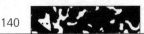

thy for reasons beyond his suggested social and political critique and proposed school and educational practice. If he were consistent with his earlier thinking and practice, we would probably not find him today supporting or promoting exclusively one strand of political or pedagogical thought or practice. Instead, we would find him, as a reflective thinker, refusing to join ideological critiques or cliques and making his own way through the contradictory and exclusionary claims people sometimes make. He would think—and think for himself. His refusal to uncritically align himself with the tides of certain progressive educational practices and particular communist political beliefs, for example, illustrates his intellectual independence. Similarly, his openness to gleaning from traditional philosophy and educational theory that which he deemed warranted demonstrates his freedom of thought. He would no doubt invite us to think for ourselves, too—even if our thinking results in partial, unsubstantiated, and mistaken conclusions at times—about largely discarded and newly enthroned educational, political, and philosophical orthodoxies and orthopraxies. His invitation must surely include his own ideas, too.

Second, there is an obvious lack of understanding or an apparent rejection of his views by many who make and enforce educational laws and policies. That is to say, the major streams of sanctioned educational reform almost uniformly disregard much that he has to say about preparing students to be reflective and ethical people. Political, policy, and business leaders rarely advance educational agendas that encourage students to reflectively engage in examining their present knowledge and interests and expanding their worlds through using their current understanding to gain new knowledge. Even less attention is devoted to supporting school activities that assist students as they learn to think about moral questions. Learning that focuses on developing a sympathy for others and insight into one's own ethical choices is poorly supported, if not vigorously discouraged. Arguments for developing a sense of democratic responsibility by students are also rare unless democracy is confused with a provincial nationalism or so-called free trade mantra. Instead, the official emphasis of many legislators, board members, and business leaders is placed largely on enabling students to learn a set of subject-specific or job-related skills and information. Reflection, if it is noted at all, runs a distant second or third for the attention of most people. The development of moral or democratic character and virtues does not usually get on the educational race track. This kind of contemporary schooling, however, does not really amount to education in Dewey's mind, for any undertaking that merits the title of education "consists in the formation of wide-awake, careful, thorough habits of thinking" (LW 8: 177).

As important as many skills and facts are, Dewey warned that beginning with such emphases neither excites learners nor encourages good teaching. To the contrary, he argued, "No one thing, probably, works so fatally against focusing the attention of teachers upon the training of the mind as the domination of *their* minds by the idea that the chief thing" is getting students to demonstrate the skills and information they have learned in a system that accents "examinations, marks, gradings, promotions" (LW 8: 164–165). The emphasis of such thinking, to underline the point, is principally upon external matters, e.g., the recognition, identification, and utilization of a set of lower-level skills and factual information. The development of the **internal abilities**—which usually have **external manifestations**—that are involved in reflection, judgment, and wisdom is unhappily missing (LW 8).

The **dominated teacher**—or the teacher whose mind and spirit is weighed down by a plethora of accountability and evaluation concerns—will probably not motivate her students frequently and regularly with a passion for learning or a hunger for fresh ideas. Why? Because thinking, questioning, probing, and evaluating are isolated from the skills and the information that provide a foundation for

---

Internal abilities

the nonpublic thought processes of students, such as imaginative rehearsal, that are often overlooked or minimized by achievement tests but are invaluable parts of reflective thinking

---

External manifestations

the external indicators of learning that are tangible evidence of easily measured student achievement

---

Dominated teacher

a teacher who is under significant ongoing pressure to prepare students to score high on achievement tests at the expense of professional judgment in the interest of student learning

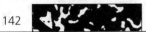

such activities. Worse still, the human and social dimensions of the information and skills learned may be ignored and schools may be stripped of "the material best suited for developing generalized abilities of thinking" (LW 8: 167). Instead, the teacher is forced to concentrate on identified information, specified skills, and prescribed outcomes. Such classroom domination, especially in the lower grades, is boring if not deadly because it divorces the student from her life, e.g., experiences, culture, and language. This is especially true if the student comes from a low-income family or a culturally different family. Regrettably, the school often focuses on what the student lacks or does not know rather than prizing what she understands. Similarly, too many school reform agendas ignore the enormous potential of using the student's current knowledge to guide her into new fields of understanding. While thinking on this topic, Dewey concluded that the development of reflective thinking is often made more difficult because upon "entering school life, a break is suddenly made in the life of the child, a break with those of his experiences that are saturated with social values and qualities. Schooling is then technical because of its isolation, and the child's thinking cannot operate because school has nothing in common with his earlier experiences" (LW 8: 167).

To make the general argument that Dewey is ignored or dismissed by many people today is not, certainly, to claim that his ideas are always or regularly correct or worth implementing. Instead, it is to assert that his questions and ideas are worth understanding as we think about educational and social matters.

A third matter that merits attention is the idea that many of the influential parties who are critical of schools are largely unaware of, indifferent to, or nonplused by the broader curricula that Dewey identified. They have very little to say about the significance of the ecological, anthropological, and pedagogical curricula, unless they are criticizing the teaching profession. As a result, these groups make at least a twofold mistake when it comes to curricular matters. First, they are narrowly if not single-mindedly concerned with the epistemological dimensions of the curriculum. Even so, studying history, chemistry, and music, even when undertaken with a cadre of marvelous teachers, will not enable children and youths to grow richly and broadly if the other dimensions of the curriculum are left to the random forces of chance and chaos. Moreover, even in the realm of the epistemological curriculum, studies are for the most part concerned with the facts and information of the official curricula—language arts, mathematics, biology, history, literature, chemistry, physics, and, at times, art, music, and theatre—and not with hidden assumptions about which subjects ought to be studied and which beliefs, interpretations, and values are warranted. While Dewey strongly supported students acquiring "a stock of knowledge," he argued that it is to be gained by guiding students into reflective inquiry, not seeing either knowledge or the mind as a static entity (LW 9: 14, 47, 61ff). So, he believed, schools should be concerned with "supplying the conditions which insure growth" toward a mature understanding, not imposing adult forms of knowledge on students (LW 9: 56).

The second mistake of those who attend largely or exclusively to the formal curriculum is their neglecting other **educational agencies** in society—the parks, coliseums, industries, banks, playgrounds, churches, malls, streets, museums, media, courts, restaurants, theatres, businesses, stadiums, and so on—that are frequently anti- and miseducative but could be educative if they were challenged and rewarded for contributing to the intellectual, emotional, ethical, political, and social development of students and society. By neglecting these other educational agencies, economically, socially, and politically powerful people—those who have the power of the streets as well those who have the power of the boardrooms—make the work of schools more difficult if not overwhelming. The limited impact of

Educational agency

any entity, such as home, church, or street corner, that is a source of teaching and learning, whether intentional or otherwise

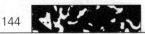

schools on the well-being of students and, thereby, on society is undermined and, at times, nullified. "Schools are," as Dewey insisted, "indeed, one important method of the transmission which forms the dispositions of the immature; but it is only one means, and, compared with other agencies, *a relatively superficial means*" (MW 9: 7; emphasis added). In actual fact, even a highly effective lightweight school is mismatched if it steps into a ring that is surrounded by a jeering crowd, overseen by an indifferent referee, and filled with a highly effective group of non-, mis-, and anti-educative heavyweights. This mismatch led Dewey in part to insist, "It would be a comparatively easy thing to educate children in an ideal way—if the parents and elders did not have to be educated first" (MW 10:116). Tragically, many "parents and elders"—often in the roles of politicians, policy-makers, professionals, business people, and action groups—believe that schools are all-powerful and that they understand better than anyone else how schools should utilize their power to revolutionize society or, more accurately at times, the economy. Equally sad is their ongoing disregard for the miseducation that occurs in their offices, chambers, businesses, homes, and neighborhoods. The education of adults, therefore, should be an ongoing concern of schools and society if we place any credence in Dewey's ideas. Imagination in pursuing this responsibility is essential.

A fourth matter that was touched upon earlier needs additional attention: Many, perhaps most, educational reform leaders—whether politicians, policy-makers, or educators—do not recognize the importance of supporting schools as they deal ethically and systematically with the values and issues of democracy. Naturally, there are many who will argue that efforts, including fiscal and programmatic ones, to ensure equality of opportunity and equity in education are designed to promote democratic ideals. They may also contend that accountability measures are intended to compel schools to guarantee that so-called low-performing schools will get the resources and programs that will provide a quality education for all students. These claims, even if well intended, can easily be contested through an analysis of empirical data. However, a Deweyan approach to this question is to some extent different and contains additional matters. From his perspective, even if there were equivalent performances on standardized measurement instruments for ethnic, racial, religious, economic, national, and gender groups, democracy has not necessarily been well served. Much more is involved in developing, sustaining, and expanding democracy. Of course, such outcomes may be greatly appreciated, especially if they were combined with a newfound respect for teachers and teaching which resulted in educators having the professional autonomy to be reflective practitioners and to conduct their own classroom activities.

Conversely, we might argue that the dreamed-of outcomes still do not prepare all groups to secure reasonably well-paying jobs, provide for the needs of their families, and to gain admission to the opportunities that are now often limited to middle- and upper-class families. We might also claim that the preparation students received would not adequately prepare them to be reflective and *"to transform a situation in which there is experienced obscurity, doubt, conflict, disturbance of some sort, into a situation that is clear, coherent, settled, harmonious"* (LW 8: 195). Students would not necessarily be prepared to operate intelligently in vocational, civic, social, and political affairs. We might also contend that schools would still not have prepared students for the responsibilities of citizenship or to value, use, and promote the values of a democracy—the freedoms of thought, press, religion, speech, assembly, so forth. Schools, we might maintain, have still failed to get students to understand and appreciate the significance of tolerance, respect, compassion, responsibility, and community. Additionally, we might argue that schools have inadequately prepared students to make practical judgments and decisions (LW 8: 210ff). Thus, we might hypothesize that the fact that there is sim-

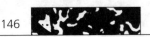

ilarity of performance on standardized achievement tests does not ensure that schools make certain that students acquire "*definite bodies of knowledge leading later to more specialized scientific knowledge*" and have become "instruments for forming alert, persistent, and fruitful *intellectual* habits" (LW 8: 290–291). In short, all students might one day do well on standardized assessment instruments and still lack knowledge of and appreciation for democratic values, governments, and living. They might also be deficient in their understanding of the bodies of knowledge, creativity, and criticism that help sustain a democracy's vitality and growth.

A final notion that deserves attention is that Dewey believed that educators should be committed to the well-being of students and society even when many in society are ill- or misinformed about the roles of schools and even when the populace—whether influential or powerful—does not highly value educating children and youths. Why is this the case? From Dewey's viewpoint, education is a moral undertaking, and professional educators are ethically responsible for preparing students to think reflectively and ethically (MW 9: 366). Professionally speaking, we enter teaching because we are committed to both teaching and learning and students and society. On one level then, we are unprofessional if we cease to work toward the best interests of students and society. Educationally speaking, our responsibility is partly based on the belief that as humans we are capable of both educating and being educated. We are capable of growing and promoting genuinely democratic schools and communities (LW 14: 226). Obviously, there are risks in trusting in ourselves and others and in democratic processes and goals, but the alternatives are usually less appealing, particularly to reflective people, educators or not. Psychologically speaking, it is self-defeating behavior to merely go through the motions of teaching and schooling. If being effective educators is challenging when we are committed to and enthusiastic about our responsibilities, we can easily speculate about the consequences of indifferent and passionless teaching. Happily, there are many who agree with Dewey's democratic and reflective emphases and who accept the challenges that come with invading "the unknown" and entering "the twilight zone of inquiry" and—Dewey would surely add—action (MW 9: 155). Becoming like Dewey—a reflective and active educational crank—may well be useful today as we work together to build educative and democratic schools and communities.

Glossary

Dominated teacher—a teacher who is under significant ongoing pressure to prepare students to score high on standardized achievement tests at the expense of her using genuinely educational experiences and professional judgment in the interest of student learning.

Educational agency—any entity (e.g., neighborhood, home, church, business, street corner) that is a source of teaching and learning, whether intentional or otherwise.

External manifestations—the external indicators of learning (e.g., on an achievement test) that are tangible evidence of easily measured student achievement.

Internal abilities—the nonpublic thought processes of students (e.g., weighing evidence, analyzing arguments, imaginative rehearsal) that are frequently overlooked or minimized by achievement tests but are invaluable parts of reflective thinking.

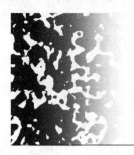

References
and Resources

Primary Resources

Boydston, J. A. (Ed.). (1967–1972). *The early works of John Dewey, 1882–1898.* (Vols. 1–5). Carbondale: Southern Illinois University Press.

_____. (Ed.). (1977). *The poems of John Dewey.* Carbondale: Southern Illinois University Press.

_____. (Ed.). (1976–1983). *The middle works of John Dewey, 1899–1924.* (Vols. 1–15). Carbondale: Southern Illinois University Press.

_____. (Ed.). (1981–1991). *The later works of John Dewey, 1925–1953.* (Vols. 1–17). Carbondale: Southern Illinois University Press.

Dewey, J. (1964). What psychology can do for the teacher. In R. D. Archambault (Ed.), *John Dewey on education: Selected writings.* Chicago: The University of Chicago Press.

Hickman, Larry. (Ed). (1996). *The Collected Works of John Dewey, 1882–1953: The Electronic Edition.* Charlottesville, VA: InteLex Corporation.

_____. (Ed.). (2005). *The Correspondence of John Dewey: The Electronic Edition.* 3 vols. Charlottesville, VA: InteLex Corporation.

Secondary Resources

Books

Biesta, G. J. J., & Burbules, N. C. (2003). *Pragmatism and educational research*. New York: Rowman & Littlefield Publishers, Inc.

Boisvert, R. (1998). *John Dewey: Rethinking our time*. Albany: State University of New York Press.

Campbell, J. (1995). *Understanding John Dewey: Nature and cooperative intelligence*. Chicago, IL: Open Court.

Cuffaro, H. K. (1995). *Experimenting with the world: John Dewey and the early childhood classroom*. New York: Teachers College Press.

Fesmire, S. (2003). *John Dewey and moral imagination: Pragmatism in ethics*. Bloomington: Indiana University Press.

Fishman, S., & McCarthy, L. (1998). *John Dewey and the challenge of classroom practice*. New York: Teachers College Press.

Fott, D. (1998). *John Dewey: America's philosopher of democracy*. Lanham, MD: Rowman & Littlefield.

Garrison, J. (1997). *Dewey and eros: Wisdom and desire in the art of teaching*. New York: Teachers College Press.

Hare, W. (1985). *In defence of open-mindedness*. Kingston and Montreal: McGill-Queen's University Press.

Hook, S. (1995). *John Dewey: An intellectual portrait*. Amherst, NY: Prometheus Books.

Jackson, P. (1998). *John Dewey and the lessons of art*. New Haven, CT: Yale University Press.

Jackson, P. (2002). *John Dewey and the philosopher's task*. New York: Teachers College Press.

Johnson, T. W. (1995). *Discipleship or pilgrimage? The educator's quest for philosophy*. Albany: State University of New York Press.

Kulp, C. B. (1992). *The end of epistemology: Dewey and his current allies on the spectator theory of knowledge*. Westport, CT: Greenwood Press.

Martin, J. (2002). *The education of John Dewey*. New York: Columbia University Press.

Maxcy, S. (2002). *John Dewey and American education*. Bristol, England: Thoemmes Press.

Mayhew, K. C., & Edwards, A. C. (1936). *The Dewey School: The Laboratory School of the University of Chicago, 1896–1903*. New York: Appleton-Century, 1936.

McDonald, H. (2004). *John Dewey and environmental philosophy*. Albany: State University of New York Press.

Menand, L. (2001). *The metaphysical club*. New York: Farrar, Straus and Giroux.

Rockefeller, S. (1991). *John Dewey: Religious faith and democratic humanism*. New York: Columbia University Press.

Ryan, A. (1995). *John Dewey and the high tide of American liberalism*. New York: W. W. Norton.

Savage, D. (2002). *John Dewey's liberalism: Individual, community, and self-development*. Carbondale: Southern Illinois University Press.

Simpson, D., & Jackson, M. (1997). *Educational reform: A Deweyan perspective*. New York: Garland Publishing.

Simpson, D., Jackson, M., & Aycock, J. (2005). *John Dewey and the art of teaching*. Thousand Oaks, CA: Sage Publications, Inc.

Tanner, L. N. (1997). *Dewey's laboratory school: Lessons for today*. New York: Teachers College Press.

Tuggle, M. (1997). *The evolution of John Dewey's conception of philosophy and his notion of truth*. Lanham, MD: University Press of America, Inc.

Welchman, J. (1995). *Dewey's ethical thought*. Ithaca: Cornell University Press.

Westbrook, R. B. (1991). *John Dewey and American democracy*. Ithaca: Cornell University Press.

Book chapters

Breese, D. (1990). The vast emergence: John Dewey. In D. Breese (Ed.), *Seven men who rule the world from the grave* (pp. 151–177). Chicago: Moody Press.

Campbell, J. (1995). Community without fusion: Dewey, Mead, Tufts. In R. Hollinger & D. Depew (Eds.), *Pragmatism: From progressivism to postmodernism* (pp. 56–71). Westport, CT: Praeger Publishers.

Carlson, A. D. (1990). The other Dewey: John Dewey, his philosophy and his suggestions to educators. In S. S. Intner & K. E. Vandergrift (Eds.), *Library education and leadership: Essays in honor of Jane Hannigan* (pp. 109–125). Metuchen, NJ: Scarecrow Press.

Hickman, L. (1996). Nature as culture: John Dewey's pragmatic naturalism. In A. Light & E. Katz (Eds.), *Environmental pragmatism* (pp. 50–72). London: Routledge.

Lavine, T. Z. (1995). America and the contestations of modernity: Bentley, Dewey, Rorty. In H. J. Saatkamp, Jr. (Ed.), *Rorty and pragmatism: The philosopher responds to his critics* (pp. 37–49). Nashville: Vanderbilt University Press.

Macke, F. J. (1995). Pragmatism reconsidered: John Dewey and Michel Foucault on the consequences of inquiry. In L. Langsdorf & A. R. Smith (Eds.), *Recovering pragmatism's voice: The classical tradition, Rorty, and the philosophy of communication* (pp. 155–176, 301–304). Albany: State University of New York Press.

Rorty, R. (1994). Dewey between Hegel and Darwin. In D. Ross (Ed.), *Modernist impulses in the human sciences, 1870–1930* (pp. 34–68). Baltimore: The Johns Hopkins University Press.

Simpson., D. (2001). The relationship of educational theory, practice, and research. In W. Hare and J. P. Portelli (Eds.), *Philosophy of education: Introductory readings* (3rd ed., pp. 29–45). Calgary: Detselig Enterprises Ltd.

Wilshire, B. (1993). Body-mind and subconscious: Tragedy in Dewey's life and work. In J. J. Stuhr (Ed.), *Philosophy and the reconstruction of culture* (pp. 257–272). Albany: State University of New York Press.

Articles

Alexander, T. M. (1993). John Dewey and the moral imagination: Beyond Putnam and Rorty toward a postmodern ethics. *Transactions of the Charles S. Peirce Society, 29,* 369–400.

Antonio, R. J., & Kellner, D. (1992). Communication, modernity, and democracy in Habermas and Dewey. *Symbolic Interaction, 15,* 277–297.

Bickman, M. (1994). From Emerson to Dewey: The fate of freedom in American education. *American Literary History, 6,* 385–408.

Blacker, D. (1994). On the alleged neutrality of technology: A study in Dewey's experience and nature. *Journal of Speculative Philosophy, 8,* 297–317.

Box, H. (1994). John Dewey: The drama of a common faith. *Religious Humanism, 28,* 11–22, 33.

Bredo, E. (1994). Reconstructing educational psychology: Situated cognition and Deweyan pragmatism. *Educational Psychologist, 29,* 23–35.

Cahan, E. D. (1992). John Dewey and human development. *Developmental Psychology, 28,* 205–214.

Callaway, H. G. (1993). Democracy, value inquiry, and Dewey's metaphysics. *Journal of Value Inquiry, 27,* 13–27.

Caspary, W. R. (1990). Judgments of value in John Dewey's theory of ethics. *Educational Theory, 40,* 155–169.

Caspary, W. R. (1991). Ethical deliberation as dramatic rehearsal: John Dewey's theory. *Educational Theory, 41,* 175–188.

Chambliss, J. J. (1994). Subject matter in John Dewey: Making objects of knowledge. *Current Issues in Education, 11,* 14–24.

Cunningham, C. A. (1994). Unique potential: A metaphor for John Dewey's later conception of the self. *Educational Theory, 44,* 211–224.

Cunningham, S. (1995). Dewey on emotions: Recent experimental evidence. *Transactions of the Charles S. Peirce Society, 31,* 865–874.

Donovan, M. (1994). Pursuing democracy as a moral task: A Deweyan response to Jeffersonian revolution. *International Studies in Philosophy, 26,* 1–11.

Duff, B. E. (1990). "Event" in Dewey's philosophy. *Educational Theory, 40,* 463–470.

Dziemidok, B. (1992–1993). Dewey's contribution to the theory of valuation. *Free Inquiry, 13,* 28–30.

Ebisch, G. A. (1994). The common faith of John Dewey. *Religious Humanism, 28,* 4–10.

Eodice, A. R. (1990). Dewey and Wittgenstein on the idea of certainty. *Philosophy Today, 34,* 30–38.

Feinberg, W. (1993). Dewey and democracy at the dawn of the twenty-first century. *Educational Theory, 43,* 195–216.

Fesmire, S. A. (1995). A dramatic rehearsal and the moral artist: A Deweyan theory of moral understanding. *Transactions of the Charles S. Peirce Society, 31,* 568–597.

Fott, D. (1991). John Dewey and the philosophical foundations of democracy. *Social Science Journal, 28,* 29–44.

Garrison, J. (1995a). Deweyan pragmatism and the episte-

mology of contemporary social constructivism. *American Educational Research Journal, 32*, 716–740.

Garrison, J. (1995b). Deweyan prophetic pragmatism, poetry, and the education of Eros. *American Journal of Education, 103*, 406–431.

Gatens-Robinson, E. (1991). Dewey and the feminist successor science project. *Transactions of the Charles S. Peirce Society, 27*, 417–433.

Giles, D. E., Jr. (1991). Dewey's theory of experience: Implications for service-learning. *Journal of Cooperative Education, 27*, 87–90.

Goodenow, R. K. (1990). The progressive educator and the Third World: A first look at John Dewey. *History of Education, 19*, 23–40.

Gouinlock, J. (1990). What is the legacy of instrumentalism? Rorty's interpretation of Dewey. *Journal of the History of Philosophy, 28*, 251–269.

Hart, C. G. (1993). Power in the service of love: John Dewey's logic and the dream of a common language. *Hypatia, 8*, 190–214.

Heinemann, H. N., & DeFalco, A. A. (1990). Dewey's pragmatism: A philosophical foundation for cooperative education. *Journal of Cooperative Education, 27*, 38–44.

Hickman, L. A. (1994). John Dewey: Philosopher of technology. *Free Inquiry, 14*, 41–43.

Hood, W. F. (1992). Technology and public action in the political philosophy of John Dewey. *Civic Arts Review, 5*, 16–19.

Hyland, T. (1993). Vocational reconstruction and Dewey's instrumentalism. *Oxford Review of Education, 19*, 89–100.

Jackson, M., & Simpson, D. (1995). Glorious dreams and harsh realities: The roles and responsibilities of the teacher from a Deweyan perspective. *Paideusis, 8* (2), 15–31.

Jackson, M., & Simpson, D. (1998). My pedagogic creed— Reflections. *The Wesleyan Graduate Review, 1* (2), 17–18.

Jacques, R. A. (1991). The tragic world of John Dewey. *Journal of Value Inquiry, 25*, 249–261.

Johnson, T. W. (1990). Philosophy as education: Reviving Dewey's vision. *Educational Foundations, 4*, 5–16.

Kahne, J. (1994). Democratic communities, equity, and excellence: A Deweyan reframing of educational policy analysis. *Educational Evaluation and Policy Analysis, 16*, 233–248.

Knupfer, A. (1993). John Dewey revisited: Multicultural educators' views on community, education, and democratic values. *Thresholds in Education, 19,* 9–15.

Leffers, M. R. (1993). Pragmatists Jane Addams and John Dewey inform the ethic of care. *Hypatia, 8,* 64–77.

Madigan, T. J. (1993). Russell and Dewey on education: Similarities and differences. *Current Issues in Education, 10,* 3–12.

Martin, K., Simpson, D., & Gallagher, J. (1998). Piaget, Dewey, and complexity. *Journal of Thought, 33* (2), 75–82.

McGee, G. E. (1994). Method and social reconstruction: Dewey's logic: The theory of inquiry. *Southern Journal of Philosophy, 32,* 107–120.

Mendell, M. (1994). Dewey and the logic of legal reasoning. *Transactions of the Charles S. Peirce Society, 30,* 575–635.

Metcalf-Turner, P., & Simpson, D. (2002). Dewey, Vygotsky and teacher preparation for urban schools. *Teacher Education and Practice, 15* (1/2), 162–175.

Miller, I. (1993). A pragmatic health care policy tradition: Dewey, Franklin and social reconstruction. *Business and Professional Ethics Journal, 12,* 47–57.

Niu, X. (1995). Mao Zedong and John Dewey: A comparison of educational thought. *Journal of Educational Thought, 29,* 129–147.

Novak, J. M. (1992). Dewey's democratic life. *Insights, 28,* 7–11.

Ostovich, S. T. (1995). Dewey, Habermas, and the university in society. *Educational Theory, 45,* 465–477.

Palermo, J., & D'Erasmo, C. (1990). Dewey and eleven-year-old thinkers: Philosophy for children at the college learning laboratory. *National Association of Laboratory Schools, 15,* 43–49.

Pappas, G. F. (1993). Dewey and feminism: The affective and relationships in Dewey's ethics. *Hypatia, 8,* 78–95.

Pratt, S. L. (1994). Two cases against spectator theories of knowledge: Lorraine Code's what can she know? and John Dewey's the quest for certainty. *Southwest Philosophy Review, 10,* 105–115.

Putnam, H. (1990). A reconsideration of Deweyan democracy. *Southern California Law Review, 63,* 1671–1697.

Radin, M. J. (1994). A Deweyan perspective on the economic theory of democracy. *Constitutional Commentary, 11,* 539–556.

Rathunde, K. (1993). The organization of energy in play and work: Dewey's philosophy of experience and the everyday lives of teenagers. *Loisir et société / Society and Leisure, 16,* 59–76.

Ratner, S. (1992a). John Dewey, E. H. Moore, and the philosophy of mathematics education in the twentieth century. *Journal of Mathematical Behavior, 11,* 105–116.

Ratner, S. (1992b). John Dewey, empiricism, and experimentalism in the recent philosophy of mathematics. *Journal of the History of Ideas, 53,* 467–479.

Reck, A. J. (1993). John Dewey's idea of ultimate reality and meaning: A mixture of stability and uncertainty in social transactions of human beings. *Ultimate Reality and Meaning, 16,* 45–55.

Reuter, R. (1993). The radical agent: A Deweyan theory of causation. *Transactions of the Charles S. Peirce Society, 29,* 239–257.

Robbins, J. W. (1994). A common faith revisited. *Religious Humanism, 28,* 22–33.

Rockler, M. J. (1993). Russell vs. Dewey on education. *Current Issues in Education, 10,* 13–23.

Rogacheva, E. (1994). Russian education in search of democracy: The relevance of John Dewey's model of the school. *East/West Education, 15,* 49–61.

Rosenbaum, S. (1994). A virtue of Dewey's moral thought. *Southwest Philosophy Review, 10,* 187–197.

Rosenow, E. (1993). Plato, Dewey, and the problem of the teacher's authority. *Journal of Philosophy of Education, 27,* 209–221.

Rosenthal, S. B. (1993). Democracy and education: A Deweyan approach. *Educational Theory, 43,* 377–389.

Rowe, W. L. (1995). Religion within the bounds of naturalism: Dewey and Wieman. *International Journal for Philosophy of Religion, 38,* 17–36.

Russell, D. R. (1993). Vygotsky, Dewey, and externalism: Beyond the student/discipline dichotomy. *Journal of Advanced Composition, 13,* 173–197.

Ryan, F. X. (1992). The Kantian ground of Dewey's functional self. *Transactions of the Charles S. Peirce Society, 28,* 127–144.

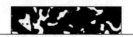

Ryan, F. J. (1993). A missing piece of the 1918 Dewey report on the Philadelphia Polish community: Mary Frances Bradshaw's ethnographic study of the Polish Catholic schools. *Records of the American Catholic Historical Society of Philadelphia, 104,* 58–78.

Ryan, F. X. (1994). Primary experience as settled meaning: Dewey's conception of experience. *Philosophy Today, 38,* 29–42.

Schön, D. A. (1992). The theory of inquiry: Dewey's legacy to education. *Curriculum Inquiry, 22,* 119–139.

Seckinger, D. S. (1994). Dewey, Martin, and the collective will: The old humanism and the new. *Teacher Educator, 30,* 43–56.

Shook, J. R. (1995). John Dewey's struggle with American realism, 1904–1910. *Transactions of the Charles S. Peirce Society, 31,* 542–566.

Shuklian, S. (1995). Marx, Dewey, and the instrumentalist approach to political economy. *Journal of Economic Issues, 29,* 781–805.

Shusterman, R. (1994a). Dewey on experience: Foundation or reconstruction? *Philosophical Forum, 26,* 127–148.

Shusterman, R. (1994b). Pragmatism and liberalism between Dewey and Rorty. *Political Theory, 22,* 391–413.

Simpson, D. (1998). Thinking about educator preparation in the 21st century: A Deweyan perspective. *Teacher Education Quarterly, 25* (4), 96–101.

Simpson, D. (1999a). John Dewey's concept of the dogmatic thinker: Implications for the teacher. *Journal of Philosophy and History of Education, 49,* 159–172.

Simpson, D. (1999b). John Dewey's view of grouping: A democratic perspective. *Educational Horizons, 77* (3), 128–133.

Simpson, D. (2001). John Dewey's concept of the student. *Canadian Journal of Education, 26* (2), 183–200.

Simpson, D. (2004). John Dewey's theory of the past, present, and future in the school curriculum. *The Review Journal of Philosophy and Social Science, 29,* 37–64.

Simpson, D., & Foley, K. (2004). John Dewey and Hubbards, Nova Scotia: The man, the myths, and the misinformation. *Education and Culture, 20*(2), 42–67.

Simpson, D., & Jackson, M. (1998). The multiple loves of the successful teacher: A Deweyan perspective. *Educational Foundations, 12,* 75–82.

Simpson, D., & Jackson, M. (2003). John Dewey's view of the curriculum in *The Child and the Curriculum*. *Education and Culture, 19* (2), 23–27.

Simpson, D., & Jackson, M. (1996). Dewey's laboratory school revisited. *The Journal of Philosophy and History of Education, 46,* 166–172.

Simpson, D., & Myers, C. (1998). Toward an ethics of communication: The importance of ethical dialogue in educational settings. *Journal of Philosophy and History of Education, 48,* 119–132.

Smiley, M. (1990). Pragmatic inquiry and social conflict: A critical reconstruction of Dewey's model of democracy. *Praxis International, 9,* 365–380.

Stever, J. A. (1993). Technology, organization, freedom: The organizational theory of John Dewey. *Administration and Society, 24,* 419–443.

Stone, G. C. (1994). John Dewey's concept of social science as social inquiry. *International Social Science Review, 69,* 45–52.

Stott, L. (1994). Dewey: A disaster. *Journal of Thought, 29,* 41–49.

Stroud, W. L., Jr. (1994). Dewey's integrated logic of science, ethics, and practice. *American Psychologist, 49,* 968–970.

Su, Z. (1995). A critical evaluation of John Dewey's influence on Chinese education. *American Journal of Education, 103,* 302–325.

Tanner, L. N. (1991). The meaning of curriculum in Dewey's laboratory school (1896–1904). *Journal of Curriculum Studies, 23,* 101–117.

Taylor, B. P. (1992). John Dewey in Vermont: A reconsideration. *Soundings, 75,* 175–198.

Teehan, J. (1995). Character, integrity and Dewey's virtue ethics. *Transactions of the Charles S. Peirce Society, 31,* 841–863.

Tiles, J. E. (1992). On deafness in the mind's ear: John Dewey and Michael Polanyi. *Tradition and Discovery, 18,* 9–16.

Wain, K. (1993). Strong poets and Utopia: Rorty's liberalism, Dewey and democracy. *Political Studies, 41,* 394–407.

Weiland, S. (1994). Erikson after Dewey: Education, psychology, and rhetoric. *Educational Theory, 44,* 341–360.

Weitz, B. A. (1993). Equality and justice in education: Dewey and Rawls. *Human Studies, 16,* 421–434.

Westbrook, R. B. (1992). Schools for industrial democrats: The social origins of John Dewey's philosophy of education. *American Journal of Education, 100*, 401–419.

Westbrook, R. B. (1993a). An innocent abroad: John Dewey and international politics. *Ethics & International Affairs, 7*, 203–221.

Westbrook, R. B. (1993b). Doing Dewey: An autobiographical fragment. *Transactions of the Charles S. Peirce Society, 29*, 493–511.

Westbrook, R. B. (1994). On the private life of a public philosopher: John Dewey in love. *Teachers College Record, 96*, 183–197.

Westhoff, L. M. (1995). The popularization of knowledge: John Dewey on experts and American democracy. *History of Education Quarterly, 35*, 27–47.

Willower, D. J. (1994). Dewey's theory of inquiry and reflective administration. *Journal of Educational Administration, 32*, 5–22.

Wilson Q. (1994). A postmodernist John Dewey? *Wilson Quarterly, 18*, 139–141.

Web site

Levine, B. (2001). Chronology of John Dewey's life and work. Carbondale: The Center for Dewey Studies, Southern Illinois University.[http://www.siu.edu/ ~deweyctr/chrono.html]